Praise for
The Ultimate Guide for New Nonprofit CEOs

Brian brings the Magic to nonprofit CEO leadership! I had the privilege of partnering with him when I represented Disney for many years on his board for the Heart of Florida United Way. Together we leveraged our combined resources to elevate our community in lasting ways. Brian is a committed, well-organized, trusted leader who made a significant difference in the lives of many Central Florida citizens. His book highlights how he made the Magic happen for his nonprofits.

– Lee Cockerell,
Executive Vice President (Retired and Inspired),
Walt Disney World Resort
Author of *Creating Magic: 10 Common Sense Leadership Strategies from a Life at Disney*

As a member of both the national and local boards of our Boys & Girls Clubs, I experienced firsthand Brian's passionate work ethic and his incredible talents as a proficient fundraising CEO. Together, we created an initiative to highlight the importance of planned giving in the charity's overall strategic plan, and the impact of our efforts were immediate and far reaching. He was also focused like a laser on improving the quality of our board and its work product, which resulted in elevating the overall charity's profile and results.

– Gary Wendt
Former Chairman and CEO,
GE Capital

As board chair during Brian's tenure at the Louisville Area Chapter of the American Red Cross, I observed, firsthand, his leadership skills in action. He adeptly led numerous natural disaster responses for Kentucky and Southern Indiana, was consistently successful at raising the necessary funds to expand our state's emergency service capacities, and was a fervent networker and collaborator throughout the community. His legacy of leadership continues today, especially in his efforts that led to the creation of an Armed Forces Emergency Services Call Center that supports our military personnel and their families here at home. Brian has a wealth of experience and proven success in the nonprofit arena, and I would urge any up-and-coming CEO to follow the powerful advice in his first book if they want to truly hit the ground running.

– Matt Bevin
62nd Governor of the Commonwealth of Kentucky

Throughout my association with Brian, I have seldom heard him use the word *I*, always deflecting praise to others and constantly looking for the next challenge, traits of a true leader. Quietly, he is a mentor to so many people, and this book will guide leaders to achieve success.

– Stephen G. Mehallis,
President,
The Harry T. Mangurian, Jr. Foundation, Inc.

Brian consistently combines his passionate leadership style and creative insights with his tactical knowledge and networking to skillfully deliver visionary new programs that enrich the community. His experience will provide insight for new nonprofit CEOs.

– Susan Burkhardsmeier
Former Executive Board Member,
Boys & Girls Clubs of Broward County

Good leaders do not do things by themselves, but they motivate others to join them to reach their vision and mission. I partnered with Brian and his team to generate support to have our shared vision become a reality. His book is your guide to leadership success as a CEO.

– Dr. Nelson Ying
Scientist, Entrepreneur, Philanthropist

As the Mayor of the City of Louisville during Brian's tenure as our Red Cross CEO, I had the pleasure of seeing firsthand his ability to bring community partners together to enact change for the citizens in our community and to serve clients beyond our city. As well as leading the charge in innumerable local disasters and city-wide challenges, Brian and I were proud to join forces to serve thousands of displaced New Orleans residents during Hurricane Katrina, which just exemplifies Brian's breadth of hearty service delivery and leadership skills. He is a strong change-agent in any community that he serves in, and his guidance in this book for new nonprofit CEOs and their boards will result in success for those who take the time to enact his strategies.

– Jerry Abramson
Former Mayor,
City of Louisville

Brian is a passionate leader who boldly took our nonprofit and its board to the next level. He put programs and procedures in place that improved our outcomes in both dollars and life-changing metrics for our kids and our community. His book will help your nonprofit establish your own metrics.

– Cathy Donnelly
Community Advocate
Former Board Chair, Boys & Girls Clubs of Broward County

Brian Quail is the rare nonprofit leader who successfully strikes the delicate balance between being a CEO charged with running a business entity and successfully managing a volunteer board, comprising community leaders and CEOs. Brian is a courageous leader willing to hold others and the organization accountable to the company's core values and mission.

– William T. Dymond Jr.
President and CEO, Lowndes

Brian is an energetic, innovative, and passionate CEO. As a board chair during Brian's tenure, I've witnessed, firsthand, his exceptional fundraising skill and his ability to motivate others, even those who, initially, felt they were uncomfortable asking for donations. Brian developed partnerships and created new programs that still exist today and continue to make a positive difference in the lives we serve. I learned a great deal from Brian and am grateful for all he did for our organization, our community, and our commonwealth. His book is a resource on how CEOs and board members can partner together in their community.

– Madeline Abramson
Former Board Chair and Life Board Member,
Louisville Area Chapter of the American Red Cross

Brian is a leader who is passionate and driven to helping those in need. I was a part of his management team for seven years witnessing his high standards along with motivating our team to be the very best. His fundraising skills and desire to create programs were based on meeting needs that were a part of our mission critical work. His book will provide you with thinking critically and analytically to be an impactful CEO.

– Emery M. Ivery
Chief Impact Officer (Retired)
United Way Suncoast

Brian was a proactive leader in addressing legal issues before they developed into major problems. As our CEO, he was always on top of reviewing important contracts and legal documents with our firm. His attention to detail and thoughtful analysis are a standard for other nonprofit CEOs to follow. His book highlights how to take these proactive steps.

– Donald B. Medalie, Esquire
Medalie & Medalie PA,
Attorneys for the Boys & Girls Clubs of Broward County, Inc.

Brian was a motivational boss who held me to extremely high standards. His energetic way of managing our staff created in me the desire to implement his practices throughout my own nonprofit executive career. I am excited for other nonprofit executives and boards to get this behind-the-scenes look at how he operates.

– Jennifer Adrio
Northeast Division Vice President, American Red Cross

Brian is a leader who inspires volunteers to go above and beyond in giving of their time, talent, and treasure—joyfully. His humble insights on how he leads are invaluable, and this book is a must-read.

– John W. Clidas, CPA/PFS, CFP, ChFC, AEP
Senior Vice President, Synovus Trust Company
Former Board Vice Chair, Boys & Girls Club of Broward County

Brian has a knowledge and understanding of nonprofit finances that most CEOs may not possess. As his finance chair, I found his understanding of nonprofit accounting and rules extremely helpful as we provided our monthly financial reports to the board and Executive Committee. New CEOs will benefit from his guidance on the importance of fiscal reporting to donors and community stakeholders.

– Vincent Palazzolo, CPA, CGMA
Former Finance Chair, Boys & Girls Clubs of Broward County

Brian Quail's advice works! He promoted me into the Resource Development Department where I developed passive income streams to deliver better ROI and offset the labor- and capital-intensive event fundraising. The assignment to diversify income, independent of the Events Department, was courageous on Brian's part since the events were championed by board members and major donors. Brian's wisdom prevailed, as relationships produced funding for club-specific activities at no cost, capital, or labor to the clubs. In addition, his efforts to consolidate fundraising, governance, and other aspects of BGCBC created parity and consistency among clubs and positioned it to survive COVID.

– Karriem Edwards
President, South Carolina Center for Fathers and Families

THE ULTIMATE GUIDE FOR NEW NONPROFIT CEOs

BRIAN QUAIL

CEO & FOUNDER OF QUAIL CONSULTING

Copyright © 2023 by Brian Quail
Quail Consulting
Fort Lauderdale, Florida

All rights reserved. No part of this book may be used or reproduced in any manner without written permission, except in the case of short quotations used for critical articles or review. Although the author and publisher have made every effort to ensure the accuracy and completeness of the information contained in this book, we assume no responsibility for errors, inaccuracies, omissions, or inconsistencies herein. Any brands, products, companies, and trademarks that appear in this book are stated for illustrative purposes only. Their mention in no way expresses explicit or implied endorsement or approval of the content in this book.

ISBN: 979-8-218-16598-7 (Paperback)
ISBN: 979-8-218-16647-2 (eBook)

Library of Congress Control Number: 2023904272

Printed in the United States of America

10 9 8 7 6 5 4 3 2 1

To my wife, Elizabeth Quail, for your unconditional support and for showing me how to hold myself to the highest of standards.

And to my daughter, Chloe Quail, the true writer of the family, for dedicating herself to her mother and our family so I could have the time to devote to this project.

Contents

Acknowledgments. xiii

Part I. Guide to Your CEO Journey 1
   Chapter 1. Welcome to Your Master Course
      in Leadership Excellence 3
   Chapter 2. What Are the Five Frameworks?. 9

Part II. A Time of Discovery 19
   Chapter 3. Framework 1: Ninety Days 21
   Chapter 4. Framework 1: Whom Do I Meet
      during My First Ninety Days? 33
   Chapter 5. Framework 1: One-on-One Meetings
      during Your First Ninety Days. 47
   Chapter 6. Framework 1: The Three Ts and Measuring
      Performance during Your First Ninety Days 71
   Chapter 7. Framework 1: Communication Protocols
      during Your First Ninety Days. 97
   Chapter 8. Framework 1: Ninety Days—
      Three Case Studies 121

Part III. Analyzing and Understanding Your Nonprofit . . . 141
　Chapter 9. Framework 2: Your Team 143
　Chapter 10. Framework 3: The Financials 165
　Chapter 11. Framework 4: Donor Relationships 193

Part IV. Bringing It All Together 225
　Chapter 12. Framework 5: The *Who* 227
　Chapter 13. Conclusion: Simple Isn't
　　the Same as Easy! 253

Notes 257
Learn More about the Five Frameworks 261
About the Author 263

Acknowledgments

MANY PEOPLE AND ORGANIZATIONS have contributed to my journey in successfully leading nonprofits. I am grateful to all. In particular, I thank:

My father, Alfred Quail, for his encouragement to use my brain and not my brawn and my mother, Betsey Quail, for raising me to lead my life with a servant heart.

The University of Massachusetts Amherst and the University of Chicago for giving me a solid foundation for all the nonprofit work I do.

All the organizations, both local and national, that have given me the rich environment in which to put my skills to their best use. I enjoyed the opportunity to serve your missions and visions throughout my career and continue to hold your work in the highest regard.

The coworkers I have had the pleasure of working with and leading. I am in your debt and cannot express my gratitude enough for your partnering with me to help bring our organizations' missions to life for the populations we served.

Through working with you, I was able to grow my leadership skills and appreciation for the tasks you executed towards our shared vision. It has been the joy of my career to have worked beside you and created the relationships and friendships that continue to sustain me to this day.

My board members and volunteers. Without the contributions of your individual talents and ideas, the missions of our organizations could never have flourished the way they did. Your leadership and guidance were the core drivers of my ability to successfully expand the reach of our work together. The lessons you gifted to me in my jobs gave me the determination and momentum to continue to improve and move forward, and therefore, any and all my successes lie within each one of you.

All my donors, funders, community partners, foundations, and fellow community nonprofit agencies for making possible all the work I did. You shared with me the insights from your own work that contributed to my overall understanding of the nonprofit world and how to navigate and lead within it.

My close friends and family. I so appreciate your continual support and encouragement while I wrote this book. Life is about balance, and you have contributed to my overall happiness and joy in ways you'll never be able to fully understand. In the moments where I encountered frustration and doubt, I was always met with wisdom and kindness that pushed me through those challenging moments. For that, I am indebted to you all. Within these pages, each of you is found.

And, last, Lawrence Ineno, my editor. I cannot express enough my deep appreciation for your patience and leadership in guiding me through this ever-complex process of bringing ideas onto the written page. You've allowed me to share my life's work with an audience in a way that will be easily accessible and impactful to those who take the suggestions within and execute them. Your presence is infused throughout the book and will eventually become a part of each future success of those who take our ideas and bring them to fruition. Thank you for your friendship.

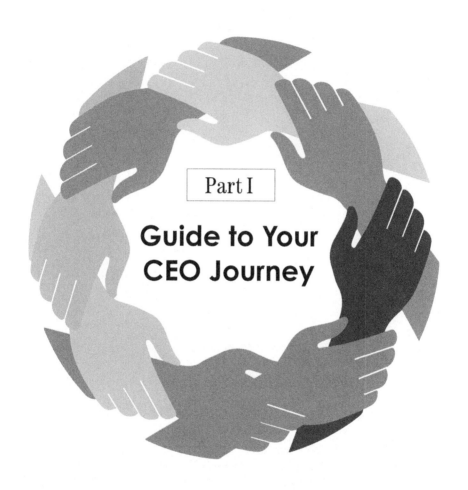

Part I

Guide to Your CEO Journey

Chapter 1

Welcome to Your Master Course in Leadership Excellence

SUCCESSFULLY LEADING THREE NONPROFITS has changed how I view what takes place around the world. From reading news about shifting political tides, natural disasters, global health crises, terrorist attacks, sweeping legislation and regulation to hearing about economic upticks or downturns, I always ask myself, "How does this event affect my nonprofit, and how do we need to respond?"

In this regard, decades heading nonprofits have turned headline news from a detached exercise in staying up-to-date to information I constantly have used to guide my leadership.

Long after leaving my last CEO post, I still haven't been able to shake the habit of interpreting current events this way. Given the direct role nonprofits play in meeting a community's most urgent and greatest need and my nearly four decades in the nonprofit sector, I'll probably always view news through an executive lens. This tendency speaks to the intensity of the work CEOs perform every day and the commitment we have to improve the lives of as many people as we can.

Rapid technological advances are improving how nonprofits serve their constituents. Cloud-based software, ever faster and more capable mobile devices, scientific breakthroughs, drones, satellite imagery, artificial intelligence, and more are rapidly improving how nonprofits deliver services to the vulnerable. At the same time, no amount of high tech will ever replace the power of one-on-one human interaction.

Walking through a community ripped apart by a natural disaster, speaking directly to caregivers who are struggling to provide for their loved ones, asking department heads and staff within the nonprofit about its strengths and weaknesses, meeting with committed donors and hearing their concerns for people, and creating connections with business and political leaders are just some of the instances where a CEO must always maintain direct lines of communication. Video conferencing, messaging, and emailing will never substitute for the nonverbal and verbal information a CEO gives and receives through face-to-face meetings.

Instilling and upholding the highest standard of communication are at the top of how new CEOs set themselves up to succeed. Unfortunately, too often I've seen otherwise capable and well-intentioned executives flounder in their roles because they haven't received thorough training in the art of communication, which points to a greater problem I've identified within nonprofits. Beyond communication are other fundamental skill sets that CEOs lack when their hiring committees give them the career-changing news, which is a variation of "Welcome aboard!"

From what I've witnessed, most nonprofits don't have a well-planned strategy to prepare their new CEOs for the enormous task ahead of them. While organizations thoroughly prepare their staff to fulfill their duties and value this responsibility, these same nonprofits neglect to address the needs of their leader. Seeing this glaring omission over time and across nonprofits was what motivated me to write this book. The Five Frameworks are the culmination of identifying the strategies and skills CEOs need to meet the nonprofit's mission and solve its most urgent problems.

If one of the top priorities of any board is to manage the CEO, then why is it that boards take a hands-off approach with their newly appointed leaders?

First, board members may not have the experience necessary to coach and guide their CEOs. Second, they may be burned out and eager to pass the burdens they carry to the new leader. Last, they may believe that once the CEO has been appointed, they can now take a step back and let him or her take over.

While all these reasons are understandable, CEOs play many roles and need tremendous support to excel in all of them. Being a sports fanatic, I love watching professional golf and playing it (I just wish my handicap was lower!). I'm always amazed at the team of professionals that top players rely on to maintain year-after-year peak performance; so many people required to make one superstar athlete compete at the highest level! From swing and strength coaches to nutritionists and sports psychologists to agents and business managers, these individuals are committed to providing pro athletes the support and resources they need to win and stay at the top.

The Five Frameworks bridge the chronic gap between boards hiring CEOs with high expectations and the practices and skills CEOs need to fulfill the obligations of their post.

Currently, "the turnover in nonprofit corner offices is between 18% and 22% annually." Given that "nonprofit executive directors and CEOs are in their roles for an average of six years, with this tenure expected to decline," board members serving the typical two consecutive three-year terms can expect to take on the onerous task of facilitating and coordinating a leadership transition at some point while on the board.

During a CEO's first year, boards are typically forgiving of tolerable degrees of underperformance or mistakes. But if downward trends continue by month eighteen, nonprofits will often show the CEO the door. For organizations that tolerate mediocrity past the year-and-a-half mark, they may do so out of lack of time or motivation or both. The executive search process is exhausting, and board members who were part of it may be disinclined to take on the burden again. Or a CEO's underachievement may reflect a flawed hiring process that resulted in a mismatch between leader and organization. Now those responsible for his or her appointment may be reluctant to acknowledge any oversights or mistakes they made. Or board members' full schedules limit how much time they can commit to the nonprofit.

When used as part of the hiring process by members of the Executive Search Committee, the Five Frameworks serve as an effective guide for assessing candidates, as well as a resource to identify the most important skills prospective CEOs must have. From day one on the job, the Five Frameworks will provide leaders a path to deliver on what they promised to bring about when they were interviewed by the hiring committee. *Thus this book is for not only CEOs but also the board members charged to oversee those leaders.*

THROUGHOUT MY CAREER, I'VE MENTORED and provided guidance to nonprofit CEOs and senior executives. I've been blessed to do work that aligns with my greatest passion: to be an entrepreneurial servant leader. Through leading nonprofits, I've touched the lives of millions of people in their time of greatest need.

When my wife, Liz, was diagnosed with a chronic health condition, our tight-knit family became closer than ever. Together with my beloved daughter, Chloe, we became a unified care team. Witnessing and benefitting from the strength and courage of the most important women in my life has inspired and lifted me up during this difficult time.

In order to take care of my wife, I stepped away from the intensity of heading a large nonprofit. With the nonstop responsibilities of being a CEO placed on hold, I've finally had the time to write this book. From late nights to the hours spent in hospitals, during periods of downtime, I flipped open my laptop. Once the screen lit up, I turned from serving as my wife's primary caregiver to being book author.

The publication of *The Ultimate Guide for New Nonprofit CEOs* comes at a time of seismic shifts that have affected the nonprofit landscape as a result of COVID-19. The workplace has changed, and communities will be affected by the coronavirus's direct and indirect aftermaths for decades to come.

During this period of uncertainty and change within nonprofits and the communities they serve, the Five Frameworks are a timeless guide for CEOs to succeed in the nonprofit business sector. While many eschew mixing nonprofits with private industry, I disagree. The concepts you'll read about are based on my belief that nonprofits should be run like businesses. Clearly, significant legal, fiscal, and organizational differences exist between the two. But many management principles that well-run corporations use apply to nonprofits as well. When nonprofit CEOs realize they are managing a business that serves the community, they understand the magnitude, scope, and responsibilities of their position.

Whether you're hired from within your organization or have been brought from outside (which was the case for my three CEO assignments), the Five Frameworks will provide the foundation you need to be a steady and strong leader, regardless of the challenges you face. This is the book I wish I had as I was solving my nonprofits' biggest problems and creating big, lasting improvements.

The insights I've imparted within these pages are based on my successful track record of dramatically improving three nonprofits and leaving a legacy within each one. My career has spanned four decades in nonprofits, including twenty-five years heading three that were part of national organizations. These nonprofits were located in major metropolitan areas with populations between 1.6 and 2.3 million people. Combined, my fundraising, oversight, analysis, and development efforts resulted in over one billion dollars in human services funding assisting millions of community members. You'll learn about fundamental practices and skills CEOs need and obstacles they face that threaten to thwart their performance, as well as how to address each one in order to tap into your greatest potential.

Working closely with their boards, great CEOs create great nonprofits, and this book is a masterclass in leadership excellence.

Chapter 2

What Are the Five Frameworks?

> **In this chapter, you'll learn:**
> - the challenges of the new CEO and how to overcome them;
> - the purpose and benefit of the Five Frameworks;
> - what **self-onboarding** is and how the Five Frameworks fill a void for nonprofits seeking leadership excellence and exceptional outcomes.

STARTING A NEW LEADERSHIP POSITION is a lot like the first day of college. When many of us look back on our university years, we remember how we felt prior to setting foot on campus at the start of the semester. We completed the admissions application and received the good news a few months later. Having made our four-year commitment, we hoped the choice was right. Saying goodbye to friends and family back home brought about sadness, anticipation, and anxiety: Will I like my new roommate? Will I make new friends and find people who are like me? Will I fit in and succeed here?

Similarly, the first day of being an executive is filled with equal amounts of excitement and fear. You may be proud that an Executive Search Committee selected you and you glided through a series of tough interviews. You're now thrilled to finally implement your ambitious vision, and at the same time, you may be terrified of failure.

You may have reached this point in your career through years of rising through the nonprofit ranks. Perhaps you started on the programs side as a staff member, providing direct service to clients. You then switched to administration, which led you to become a director, followed by vice president, and now CEO. Or you may be an outsider. While nonprofits have traditionally hired and promoted those within, appointing leaders beyond organizational walls has been a recent trend. As we've seen in multiple industries, many of today's leaders move from one organization to another. Some may even transition from for-profit to nonprofit leadership. Or like me, you may have earned a master's degree, begun work first as a budget analyst and then an entry-level fundraiser, and continued moving to the top, becoming CEO of different nonprofits.

No matter how many times over the decades I've successfully turned around struggling organizations or improved thriving ones, all of them were in need of major improvements. Starting in a new position still gives me those first-day-of-school jitters.

The person at the highest level, who reports to and directly works with the board of directors and is overseen by the board of directors, its chair, and the Executive Committee, has different titles, depending on the organization. You may be a CEO, an executive director, or president/CEO. Whatever the label, the buck stops with you. To simplify, throughout this book, I'll refer to this person as CEO.

Harvard Business Review reported that *one-third to one-half of new CEOs fail in their first eighteen months on the job.* WOW! That telling statistic is one reason that motivated me to put leaders on the path to success through the Five Frameworks. When CEOs are let go due to underperformance or not being the right fit, their failure and ensuing organizational disruption ripples through the organization.

The following are why nonprofit CEOs and the organizations they lead fail. While one of these items may be the only reason that results in an organization's breakdown or having to make a CEO change, oftentimes a combination of factors is the cause:

1. **A CEO's insufficient skill set.** Human resources, finance, resource development, building and maintenance, program and direct service, community donors, and more ... a leader must understand all the organization's operations, including the strengths and weaknesses within its departments. Does the CEO know how to read financial statements, what it takes to close the books each month to produce financial statements, the role of a quality constituent relationship management (CRM) system, and how fundraising staff effectively use it?
2. **Conflicts between CEOs and boards.** Such disagreements often arise when division of responsibility is not clear or duties overlap. A healthy division of labor between the CEO and his or her board is necessary for the nonprofit to fulfill its long-term mission. The CEO effectively develops and executes strategies, and the board is responsible for advising and approving the work. In addition, each group must have clarity regarding its

role in making decisions and what must be carried out to meet an organization's desired expectations.

3. **Not clearly stating the organization's mission, purpose, and structure.** From agency program staff to the person charged to clean the building, all employees must be in alignment, which means your nonprofit team fully understands the organization's mission, purpose, and structure. The team does so by following the leader's cue. For nonprofits that are part of a national organization, alignment includes complying with membership standards.

4. **Not educating volunteer leadership and staff about the revenue streams.** When volunteer leadership and staff understand how the nonprofit generates income, this means they clearly understand how the organization raises money, supports programs, and generates revenue or the requirements attached to funding streams, including mandatory reporting. As a result, the team becomes an effective part of the nonprofit's public fundraising efforts.

5. **Unpredicted and sudden revenue losses.** For example, donors may stop supporting an organization, or grants may discontinue for any number of reasons, including broad economic downturns such as what took place after 2008's global financial crisis.

6. **An outdated or non-existent long-term strategic plan.** Within an organization and in the world at large, change is constant: The economy tanks, natural disasters and pandemics occur, and new government regulations are enacted. Yesterday's plans become obsolete and need to be continually reevaluated and updated for relevancy.

When an organization has a current long-term strategic plan, it is prepared to address future needs and clearly articulated desires for success, which includes pragmatic objectives, as well as big, audacious ones.
7. **Poor financial practices.** An organization's fiscal health is the primary pillar of its long-term success. Organizations must have accounting procedures and policies, solid money management practices, and financial oversight.
8. **Inadequate technology infrastructure.** In order for a nonprofit to maintain its longevity, it must keep up with technology, which never stops improving, and provide adequate reserves for new equipment and upgrades. Allocating funds to technology is difficult for many organizations but should be a priority.

Furthermore, hiring a CEO is *a lot* of work! In my experience, hiring committees spend six to ten months finding the right leader. No wonder those serving on the hiring committee are often exhausted and burnt out once their duty is done. The months of hard work on the part of volunteers wind up curbing their enthusiasm during a time that should otherwise be a cause for celebration.

In many instances, over a year passes between a prior CEO leaving and the new one filling the vacant post. During this interim phase, employees, volunteers, and donors may lose confidence in the nonprofit, and even worse, donations may decrease. Like a computer's safe mode, everyone seems to be limping along, waiting to size up the new executive and, more importantly, to see if the board of directors will support the new CEO.

Given the challenges new CEOs and their nonprofits face, it's clear why so many CEOs fail to meet the ambitious promises they made that led to their appointment by the hiring committee. In fact, according to a 2019 PwC study, "Successors to long serving CEOs are not faring as well as they are likely to have shorter tenures, worse performance and more often forced out of office than the CEOs they replaced." Thus the hiring committee's good intentions and long hours of hard work may only have provided a short-term fix. But the good news is failure is avoidable and success is in your hands! The Five Frameworks are a CEO's roadmap to exceptional leadership with equally extraordinary outcomes.

Self-Onboarding Fills a Void for CEOs within Nonprofits

IN CORPORATE SPEAK, **ONBOARDING** IS IMMERSING a new employee into the organization with a consistent message. This assimilation process can last three months to a year, and the initial nonprofit orientation is part of it. Orientations are short, sometimes one-time events and one-way, which means a facilitator instructs the newcomer. Onboarding is a long-term two-way collaboration between the new person and individuals well steeped in the organization's procedures, history, and culture. This method conveys the belief new employees are part of a winning team and the organization is committed to their success.

Throughout my academic and professional career, I constantly learned about the importance of onboarding. Having a clear and comprehensive strategy to introduce new people into the organization is a fundamental step to create consistency throughout the nonprofit.

Onboarding forms the foundation of strong teamwork, which is essential to nonprofit excellence. Think of onboarding as teaching the newcomer the organization's playbook, which includes a guide to jargon within the industry and the nonprofit itself, as well its history, procedures, vision, mission, and values. Each new person has his or her own history, strengths, and weaknesses. Despite the differences we all have, onboarding ensures we share a common language that is fundamental to a nonprofit fulfilling its mission and for CEOs to realize their ambitious vision.

Without a doubt, having an onboarding process is a non-negotiable no-brainer. If the nonprofit you were just hired to lead doesn't have an onboarding process for new employees, implementing one will be one of your top priorities. While onboarding is essential for everyone within your nonprofit, what about you, the person at the top?

After an unending succession of sleepless nights caring for their crying newborn, you'll often hear first-time parents say some variation of "No one gave me a handbook for this!" Similarly, upon entering my CEO assignments, although some of my nonprofits had a thorough onboarding process for staff, others did not for me as CEO. While national organizations I was affiliated with over my career brought new leaders together in the first year to their headquarters, it was an orientation, rather than onboarding as defined in this section. For the immense amount of content and discussion you'll find about onboarding and how critical it is to a nonprofit's efficacy, I've always found it amusing that when it comes to onboarding CEOs, we leaders are frequently left to fend for ourselves.

From what I've seen, even if a nonprofit's board has what it calls onboarding for CEOs, it's more a glorified orientation. I believe everyone assumes a CEO arrives fully prepared, trained, with all necessary skills, and thus without a need for onboarding. Whatever the case, the lack of CEO onboarding is one example among many of why so many CEOs fail in their first eighteen months.

The Five Frameworks are a CEO's **self-onboarding** process that fills the void resulting in underperformance. Without self-onboarding, one can surmise why CEOs are often hired with great enthusiasm and optimism but months later fail to meet expectations, to the chagrin of everyone within the nonprofit including its struggling leader. Indeed, CEOs require a specific set of tools and skills that no one else in the organization requires, and the Five Frameworks tackle these head on.

This self-onboarding process, as you'll learn in the subsequent chapters, can take a year, and the first three months are the most important, which is why part 2, "A Time of Discovery," focuses on those critical ninety days and comprises six chapters. Next, in part 3, "Analyzing and Understanding Your Nonprofit," you'll learn about Frameworks 2 through 4, each with its own subsequent chapter directed specifically to targeted objectives you must learn in your first year as CEO. Last, in part 4, "Bringing It All Together," you'll learn how to apply everything you've read in order to tap into your greatest leadership potential.

Together, all Five Frameworks are the building blocks of your leadership. In the short-term, they are your self-onboarding process that comprise straightforward tasks requiring your undivided time and attention and months to complete. In the long-term, as the years progress during your tenure, the five give you immense freedom to dream big and see the tangible results of your vision for yourself and your nonprofit. Thus every minute you spend completing each task and mastering each skill set within the Five Frameworks will save you immeasurable time and spare you from facing countless obstacles—many that could be career killers—later.

I'll go into much more depth in the following pages, but for now, here's an easy way to remember each of the Five Frameworks:

Framework 1: Ninety Days
Framework 2: Your Team
Framework 3: The Financials
Framework 4: Donor Relationships
Framework 5: The *Who*

While they're presented as one through five, these are not step by step. In other words, you don't master one Framework and move on to the next. Rather, each one describes a skillset you need for peak performance. Like a building's structural columns, you require the support of each, so you can't skip any. With the checklists, recommendations, and real-world examples I provide in each, you'll be referring to sections over and over and determining how to apply these lessons to your everyday responsibilities.

The Five Frameworks are both a practical guide and audaciously ambitious roadmap to high achievement. Work on them concurrently, and once you've mastered them all, the Five Frameworks are the foundation of your leadership legacy. By following them with fastidious commitment, I guarantee you will be successful: You will unleash your potential to elevate your nonprofit and your performance beyond what's otherwise possible.

Part II

A Time of Discovery

Chapter 3

Framework 1: Ninety Days

> **In this chapter, you'll learn:**
> - the importance of your first ninety days on the job and how Framework 1 provides you a roadmap to establish your leadership within your nonprofit and the community it serves;
> - the art of delegating and strategies to master in order to reach the ninety-day targets outlined in Framework 1;
> - how one-on-one meetings coupled with storytelling provide you with insight about the organization, win others' support of your plans, and pave the way for your success.

As you read Framework 1, it may feel like a tall order. It is. Your to-do list is already longer than you'd probably like to admit and growing lengthier by the moment. From day one on the job, newly appointed CEOs face a steep learning curve.

When in doubt, remind yourself that you're up to the challenge. You chose this path of leadership, and now's your time to shine and take your nonprofit to the next level! Always remember to have fun learning and growing as you implement your ideas and vision for the future.

You're a troubleshooter, charged to identify your nonprofit's strengths and weaknesses and solve urgent problems. Now, on top of your near endless to-do list, Framework 1 says to arrange and meet with various groups—both in big settings and personal one-on-one appointments—within ninety days. By doing so, you'll demonstrate how your leadership signals a wonderful era for the organization, one that will bring it to new heights, attaining its vital mission, and set the tone of your new leadership tenure.

So why ninety days? In my experience, three months gives new executives enough time to identify and then complete all the tasks most valuable to their organization. Also, determining and then sticking to deadlines are an effective strategy to goal attainment. A ninety-day deadline generates the right amount of pressure to keep you driving toward the finish line: It's not unreasonably short, which is a formula for failure, and it's not too long, which can lead to losing focus and urgency on the leader's part and a diminished overall impact of the achievement once it's reached. People have short attention spans, and the excitement surrounding your recent appointment will eventually fizzle. A ninety-day accomplishment will carry forward the momentum you've built and will remind your board, staff, volunteers, and community why you are ideally suited to head the organization.

The Importance of One-on-One Interactions and Storytelling

FRAMEWORK 1 IS THE FAST TRACK to immersing yourself in your nonprofit. This is my favorite Framework because its primary purpose is to earn you credibility and goodwill within the organization that reflect you're ideally suited to be its leader. Establishing trust as early as possible is essential and facilitates meeting the ambitious goals you have for your nonprofit. Neglect to build trust quickly, and you are setting yourself up for failure in your leadership role. Framework 1 builds trust within a short timeframe. By doing so, you make your job easier and your leadership role more effective going forward.

Completing the tasks as you head toward the ninety-day mark will provide you information about your organization and the communities it serves that you would otherwise not have received.

Framework 1 is an evaluation tool. You are digging deeply within the nonprofit, gaining far more information than what will appear in a report or another person's account. With your own two hands, you're immersing yourself into your nonprofit faster and more effectively than otherwise possible, asking questions, and receiving answers that give you profound insight. You are learning the history of the organization beyond what is published about it. As a result, you're drawing conclusions based on what you see and hear from speaking with those most closely connected with your nonprofit's mission. By doing so, you will be able to accurately evaluate the quality of the nonprofit's people, processes, and systems. You'll uncover problems that have been neglected, avoided, or even hidden.

Through this exhaustive discovery phase, you will determine where to focus your short- and long-term efforts, as well as learn what those within and outside your nonprofit expect you to accomplish. Framework 1 is a fact-checking exercise. You are verifying whether the information you were given about the nonprofit aligns with your personal assessment.

I loved all the vital face-to-face conversations I had with those inside and outside the organization as I worked my way through Framework 1. Progressing through the ninety-day plan, I always found the staff, volunteers, and donors appreciated my commitment. My efforts showed them that, as its new CEO, I was engaged with and wanted to learn about every aspect of the enterprise. They appreciated that I was seeing their role, including their concerns and needs, through their perspectives. By viewing the nonprofit through their points of view, I also learned a great deal about it. Working through the steps of Framework 1 made my presence known throughout all levels of the nonprofit. Staff, the board, and donors saw how my leadership signaled a bright, new day for the enterprise and the people we served.

Inside the organization, you'll gain an intimate look into how your staff and volunteers at the board level and those who deliver services within departments conduct their work. Through these meetings, you'll be able to assess the quality of the operation and how the staff react to you.

By meeting the staff, I was able to observe firsthand the demeanor of those who directly reported to me. Every nonprofit has its own organizational structure. What I'll refer to as **direct reports** in this book may go by different names in your organization—senior executive, senior management team, internal department heads, or department leaders—and they may have titles such as executive vice president, director, or non-CEO C-level designations such as chief of operations, technology, or finance.

Organizations are like people; each one has its own personality. You may be CEO of a single-location nonprofit or the leader of one with multiple locations, each of which has its own leaders. While in both cases, face-to-face meetings are essential, the larger and more complex your organization is, the more meetings you'll have. Within each site, the staff culture is different, as is the demographic makeup of its clients. Perhaps one operation's client base is 70 percent one ethnic group. Meanwhile, another location in another part of the county may consist of 60 percent of another ethnic group. When CEOs of nonprofits with multiple operations take in-person tours of each site, this gives them the opportunity to learn about the operation's leader, its volunteers and employees, and its clients. These key connections will benefit CEOs in the short and long term.

For example, you may recognize why one location follows operating guidelines better than another. Or you may see that one site raises more money and has higher volunteer support than another. Through your in-person meetings, you realize the reason behind the more successful operation's accomplishments.

Outside the organization, Framework 1 requires you to leave the four corners of your office and hit the streets in order to receive firsthand knowledge of the community your organization serves.

Skillful communication is one of the hallmarks of a strong leader. As a CEO, you're selling nonstop. Whether it's an ambitious plan you're pitching to your team, board, and community; an appeal to a potential donor; seeking funding from local government entities that benefits your nonprofit's constituents in the community; asking for volunteers from a local company to strengthen your organization's community involvement image; or reaching out via social media with videos and texts regarding the nonprofit's work, the primary way you communicate using your powers of persuasion is through masterful storytelling.

One objective of your ninety-day initiative is to collect compelling and inspiring stories you've heard from day one via the long list of people you've met inside and outside your organization. The interactions you've had through your face-to-face meetings are the real-life experiences you'll refer to when communicating with others. Among the wide range of stories you've amassed within this short timeframe, you'll determine which ones will best illustrate your point, resonate with your audience, and serve your purpose when you're communicating with them.

In the age of Zoom and texting, we can easily think online meetings are the same as in-person ones. But they are not. The 2020 global lockdowns as a consequence of the coronavirus demonstrated the power and limitations of technology. Professionals across the world were able to continue working and supporting themselves and their families by working from home via the internet. But results did not always match pre-lockdown standards. For example, K through 12 student performance tanked because of online learning.

Human communication is both verbal and non-verbal. Many non-verbal cues are lost when a person is shrunk to a monitor or tablet screen that shows only his or her face. Many body language signals are completely lost in most video meetings. While online meetings play an important role within an organization, they are no substitute for in-person interactions.

Visiting sites, I would immediately be able to assess the workplace climate. When the location's leader and I walked through the facility, I observed how staff and volunteers reacted to us. If they seemed to avoid interaction or were reluctant to join in, this was always a sign of concern. And if they were eager to see us and welcomed our presence, this was always a good sign. I also looked to see if buildings were clean and cared for properly and noted any necessary capital improvements.

Because I was the boss, people were often yes men and women. In other words, they told me what they thought I wanted to hear versus what they thought I needed to know. But sometimes people broke from this tendency and expressed their true opinion in hopes to benefit the nonprofit. This honesty demonstrated their commitment to improving their clients' lives.

During one site visit, a team member told me, "We're so proud of the program we run here, but one issue is the technology we use for the kids." The person then showed me how half of the computers serving the youth were too outdated to load the new math and reading software ordered to tutor the children. At the same time, the old machines were still useful because the youth without computers at home were able to practice keyboarding skills on them. I noted input like this as well. Problems I observed or were pointed out to me could also generate other questions I would ask myself or, when appropriate, staff, such as "How come these computer labs haven't been upgraded?" and "Does the organization have a computer replacement program? If not, then it's time to implement a plan to keep the computer lab up-to-date." My search for answers would lead to finding more about the strengths and weaknesses of the organization. Videoconferencing cannot provide such an expansive and hands-on view of how an organization operates.

Sometimes an improvement that needed to be made was simple, and the expense could be justified over time. For instance, a room's dimness can be solved by upgrading and installing new electrical ballasts to accommodate better lighting. A simple change done quickly may seem insignificant, but your combined big and small efforts send a strong message of your commitment to your staff's wellbeing. Remember that, while staff satisfaction is certainly linked to pay, many other factors such as recognition for a job well done, a positive and uplifting workplace, and supervisors who demonstrate they care, all expressed in tangible and intangible ways, engender staff loyalty.

Imagine you're on your smartphone and receive news about a local natural disaster that has struck your city and has resulted in fires and destruction of property. You watch videos and thumb through images detailing the devastating event. Compare that online experience with witnessing the tragedy's aftermath in person.

You arrive at the scene. You smell the smoke in the air. You see the ashes floating around you. Beneath your feet, you feel the rubble from houses now flattened and hear the sobs of residents who have lost their homes. Without insurance, they have no place to stay the night, let alone a house to live in anymore.

Being a CEO is stressful work, and some days I felt defeated. But after visiting a site and seeing its community programs in action, I always realized how fortunate I was. My professional struggles at any given moment in my career paled in comparison to the trauma I often witnessed others experience. Observing team members serving clients such as youth in afterschool programs, running a shelter during a disaster, or conducting CPR trainings, I saw the direct result of the work I did to generate funding and lead a healthy organization. Seeing the powerful work the nonprofits I ran did to improve communities and the lives of those within them recharged my batteries and motivated me to fulfill their mission. As a result of your on-the-scene visit, you too will feel deep within yourself what the people must be experiencing.

Looking people eye-to-eye builds empathy, allows you to offer it to others, and gives you a perspective into their feelings at the moment that no amount of screen time can replicate. The real-life accounts you gather through your one-on-one interactions will collect like chapters in your book of nonprofit stories. They remind you of why you chose this professional path and feed the passion that drives you to work hard to improve the organization and community you serve. In addition, your physical presence lends credibility to your leadership. Once you give up being present, you're sending the message "I don't care." Intentional or not, your actions will influence your organization's climate. On the one hand, when you don't visit sites, you create an us-versus-them culture. This causes a distance and even hostility between the main office and the locations outside it. On the other hand, when you visit sites consistently, it encourages the staff of each one to be accountable in upholding the nonprofit's mission, and it demonstrates your interest in its success.

When you're addressing a group, you'll refer to stories that illustrate the data and facts for those driven by their heads.

These people want numbers and analysis. You'll refer to stories that support the lives and experiences for those driven by their hearts. These folk want to identify with people in need. By combining the head and heart, you tell a complete story to donors who are asking themselves why your organization deserves their support and why you need it.

Delegate to Push You across the Ninety-Day Finish Line

As the days and weeks quickly pass, where you wish every day had more than twenty-four hours in it, earning credibility through arranging and meeting with various groups—both in big settings and personal one-on-one appointments—within ninety days is a major feat that will earn the trust and respect of those around you. They will see you as a person of action who desires to learn from what has taken place within the nonprofit prior to your appointment. Nonprofit staff, and particularly long-term employees, are often proud of what they've accomplished and the role they've played in the organization's evolution, history, and achievements. When newly appointed leaders appreciate the nonprofit's legacy and the key individuals who have been part of it, they are doing their part to earn credibility and respect.

Having a team of highly motivated people on your side is how you'll bring about the results you seek. This includes your board, who see the actions you are taking are based on your exhaustive inquiry and evaluation of the nonprofit. Earning credibility through one-on-one meetings forms the foundation of the Frameworks that follow. In this regard, because this

Framework is the basis of the other four, it is the most important. Thus, develop a timeline on how you will achieve the desired objective to begin your new leadership role to meet the objective of Framework 1.

Accomplishing Framework 1 will take commitment and discipline. While the work is substantial, the benefits will make all the time and energy you spent worthwhile. Also, keep in mind that you will not be alone. Delegating tasks to your direct reports is an important part of this Framework. Many of the tasks you'll read about require others to help you reach what will be a defining moment in your leadership tenure. Through delegation, you'll learn more about those within your organization and how they work together as they join you on this remarkable ride.

One of the outcomes of meeting your ninety-day goal is it helps you build your team; part of building your team requires you to engage with your staff and, specifically, your direct reports on a one-on-one basis, where you'll listen to their perspectives about their programs and departments.

CEOs can come into a position with prior experience that leads them to believe they're able to assess on their own what an organization needs. But if they drop any pre-existing belief that they have a firm grasp of the nonprofit, the hands-on work of in-person meetings will shed light on new information far beyond what appears in an annual report or Search Committee interview. This is why I emphasize in-person meetings and site visits are best. The approach here is to establish not what you already know as the new CEO about the organization but what you need to know about the organization that is beyond what is public and readily accessible.

Chapter 4

Framework 1: Whom Do I Meet during My First Ninety Days?

> **In this chapter, you'll learn:**
>
> - the importance of face-to-face meetings—both group and one-on-one—and how they are essential for all your nonprofit's clients such as staff, board of directors, donors, and community leaders;
> - how to host casual and fun group meetings that allow you to see the personalities and group dynamics within your staff, connect with your team, and gain credibility;
> - effective strategies to conduct in-depth, one-on-one meetings that reveal your direct report's expertise, uncover your nonprofit's history and otherwise hidden stories, and establish a solid relationship with your donors.

THE AFTERMATH OF THE GREAT CRASH in 2008 decimated nonprofits across the country. Funding dried up, and organizations had to cut staffing. In the case of my nonprofit, it had dismissed over forty employees before I arrived. With low employee morale and the broader economy in peril, I was charged to figure out how to move forward. Under these dire circumstances, I decided to meet with our nonprofit's funders. If we wanted to bounce back from this, we needed to understand the perspective of those who held a large part of our fate in their hands via their contributions. Through this process, I learned the specific belt-tightening measures these funders were performing within their own organizations, as well as the burdens they carried. I gained a clear understanding behind why they had to reduce their support of nonprofits, including ours.

Both the funders and I headed our organizations. Thus, we understood how each of us had to make tough choices during this crisis. Those meetings I organized during the worst of the financial crisis opened doors for me when the global economy began showing signs of recovery. The CEOs of these funding organizations appreciated the time I had spent identifying their biggest obstacles. When I believed their organizations were ready, I asked them for their financial support. Most resumed their contributions to pre-financial-crisis levels, and some even gave beyond their prior pledges.

This example points to the importance of face-to-face meetings. Determining whom you must meet with inside and outside your nonprofit during your first ninety days is key to accomplishing this ambitious task. I've led organizations that had from seventy to one hundred full-time employees and from fifty to one hundred fifty part-time employees. Coordinating so many schedules was never easy, but meeting and deepening your connection with your full-time staff is your first focus.

Within your nonprofit are your direct reports and their departments, which comprise both full-time and part-time staff. Given the high number in the organization and their work hours, coordinating so many schedules may not be possible, so do what is feasible.

Outside your organization are your individual donors, foundations, corporate sponsors, and government funders, along with your current board of directors, past board chairs, and founding members. Plus, you'll have others, based on your organization's specific needs and characteristics.

Next, within your organization, your ninety-day goal comprises one-on-one and group meetings of full-time staff. Your one-on-one meetings will be with your direct reports and the professionals who directly report to them. Depending on the organization, these professionals may be called directors, senior directors, assistant vice presidents, or area directors. Within your nonprofit, you may use other titles associated with this level of professional responsibility. During these meetings, you'll have in-depth discussions where you'll explore in detail aspects of their individual roles, as well as the state of their departments.

The following are those you'll meet with and, as the list shows with your direct reports, some you'll meet with more than once:

Group meetings inside your nonprofit
- Direct reports or senior executive team
- Director level staff
- Full-time staff of each department

Internal leaders
- Direct reports or senior executive team

External customers
- Board members
- Past board chairs
- Founding members or their families
- Past executives of the organization if appropriate

Group Meetings
Inside Your Nonprofit

BECAUSE GROUP MEETINGS ARE DONE in a bigger setting, you'll complete this item on your list quickly. Each nonprofit has its own organizational structure. One nonprofit may comprise five departments of various sizes ranging from five to fifty employees in each. This was the case for the large nonprofits I led. Administrative departments have twelve full-time employees at most, but usually an administrative department size ranges from five to ten full-time staff. Meanwhile, direct service departments have more than twelve because they include staff that carry out client-program services, which is the nonprofit's primary mission. Given the major proportion of an organization's budget allocated toward client service, the direct-client service departments are always larger than administrative departments. Thus arranging meetings with these large departments requires coordinating multiple schedules. To add to the difficulty of setting up appointments with big groups, a nonprofit may operate multiple sites within a geographic area, such as within a state or county.

In order to meet with all full-time staff within a complex organizational structure that may have large departments spread across multiple sites in different locations, consider seeking the support of your department's direct report. **Work together to cap each meeting at twelve people. If your department exceeds this number, then have more than one meeting.** Five to twelve participants per meeting usually took me about ninety minutes, which gave us enough time to have meaningful dialogue. Through your planning, you may decide to meet by geographic areas or groups of employees who work in the same location. For example, you may organize your meetings into northern, central, and southern areas.

While the one-one-on meetings with your direct reports that you'll learn about in this chapter will be technical and require participants to demonstrate their expertise within their departments, group meetings are the opposite. These are casual, light, and fun—similar to guests talking to each other in your home. This is a cocktail hour with no cocktails. They are a way to introduce yourself on a personal level to individual departments, which means some people will meet with you twice: Your direct reports and those who directly report to them will meet you one-on-one and in this group setting.

In a variation of the saying "if you build it, they will come," experience has taught me that if you serve food, they will come and enjoy the meeting even more. I have arranged breakfasts, provided pizza lunches, and hosted ice cream socials. Either out of my own pocket or by receiving permission from my board chair to use funds from the operating budget, I found a way to pay for these meetings. I would always let my team know who was footing the bill because this gained goodwill from them and it showed my commitment to transparency.

As the newly appointed CEO, I enjoyed hosting these sessions to meet my new team. My email invites went out a week in advance and would take into account the size of each department. For example, one of my nonprofits had five departments with sizes ranging from five to forty-five employees. By hosting these events with no more than twelve people in each session, I was able to meet them in the conference room next to my office.

In addition, because my nonprofit had multiple sites, I held some meetings in remote locations throughout the county. For example, the full-time staff providing direct client services in locations across the county work from noon to 8:00 p.m. Unlike the smaller administrative departments where an afternoon ice cream social would be easy to schedule, the same event would not work for staff providing direct client services who are fixed to their posts serving clients. Because of the size of the Direct Service Department, its locations across the county from my office, and the staff's schedule, I worked closely with each department head. By coordinating with my direct reports for each meeting, I was being thoughtful about each department's schedule. So I, along with my executive assistant and the department head, determined the type of lunch (which was usually pizzas or subs) with the meeting to start before noon (which was the best time). So rather than an afternoon ice cream social, we planned a ninety-minute lunch from 11:00 a.m. to 12:30 p.m. at the site itself.

Whether the meeting was an ice cream social, pizza lunch, or breakfast, the setup was the same: On a projector screen were seven questions broad enough to not feel invasive and specific enough to motivate participants to share details that expressed their personalities and interests:

1. What are your name and nickname, if you have one?
2. What is your title?
3. How long have you been with the organization?
4. What are your roles and responsibilities in the department?
5. What are your hobbies?
6. Do you have a favorite sports team?
7. What's the most exciting trip you've ever taken?

Questions 2, 3, and 4 are related to their work. The last three are about who they are beyond their job description, which let me get to know the team beyond what is appropriate to ask during a job interview. My objective was to learn aspects of their lives that they wished to share with me. To encourage and steer them in the right direction, I modeled what I sought by describing details about my personal life.

Thus I started each meeting by answering the seven questions, and I would weave my personal and professional background into my answers. Hearing about my family, my favorite sports teams, and where I grew up during my childhood put my new employees at ease. Participants remembered my responses, and I remembered theirs long after the meeting. While I answered each of the seven, I did not stick strictly to the questions because, as with any natural conversation, details emerge unrelated to the question at hand.

I used this exercise in every organization I led to observe how each team member responded not just to me but also to each other. Employees sometimes learned things about their co-workers that they did not know before. I always took notes during these meetings, and I let my employees know my note taking was a way for me to keep track of the many people I would be meeting over the next few weeks. Rather than express concern, some joked about it, reflecting they didn't mind. I observed times department members helped each other out, especially those who were introverts and did not enjoy public speaking. I always appreciated seeing this camaraderie because it showed that the department members supported each other.

These meetings were part of how I introduced my leadership style to the team. While I was their boss first, I also wanted to connect with them as individuals. My implicit message to them was "I'm expecting you to work hard. At the same time, get ready to have a blast as we serve the community together!" They were my work family, and as such, I created a professional culture rooted in respect, clear communication, discipline, fun, and kindness.

Every session I concluded by describing how I enjoyed getting to know each participant and then detailed my three-month goal of meeting with each department, donor, corporate sponsor, foundation leader, board member, and other important stakeholders to the organization. You'll learn about how to conduct these meetings throughout Framework 1.

I described these appointments with the team, particularly the ones with the big donors, which earned me credibility and a vote of confidence from the group. Other objectives for the next ninety days I outlined included learning about each department head's internal leaders and our nonprofit's external customers. Internal leaders are the heads of departments. External customers are clients, donors, and stakeholders. These include your organization's partners, individual and corporate donors, the board of directors, foundation and community leaders, founding members, past board chairs, and past executives too.

Providing this summary was a high-impact way to close a seemingly lightweight and casual meeting. The attendees appreciated the direction I was taking, the importance I placed on their role within the nonprofit, and how, as the new CEO, I was hitting the street: I would be meeting not only them but also those who were helping us make a difference.

Before the session concluded, I always asked for any questions from the group. By checking in, I was encouraging them to have open and honest conversations with me moving forward.

I also took the opportunity in my closing to let them know I might need their help to prepare for these high-level meetings with donors. By doing so, I was also informing them that they would soon be receiving requests for two reasons. First, I would use the information they would provide to prepare for important meetings with stakeholders. Second, I would also use it for later one-on-one meetings with department heads. Prior to these appointments, I provided them in-depth questions about their departments.

These department meetings gave me a broad overview of the nonprofit. In contrast, the one-on-one meetings provided me an in-depth view of the nonprofit's moving parts. The questions department heads received would require responses showing expert competence in their roles. Their answers gave me the information I needed to evaluate the quality of their leadership and department. I would know precisely what each head did and didn't know about his or her department and his or her skill level—the depth and complexity of the questions meant I'd quickly spot inadequate answers.

Internal Leaders

As you meet with entire teams during your first ninety days, you'll also have in-depth one-on-one meetings with your direct reports. These are the leaders of each of your nonprofit's departments: Human Resources, Finance, Resource Development, Communications and Marketing, Building and Maintenance, and Program/Direct Service Delivery. In chapter 5, you'll learn essential questions to ask your direct reports.

External Customers

THESE INCLUDE YOUR ORGANIZATION'S PARTNERS, individual and corporate donors, the board of directors, foundation and community leaders, and others identified as part of the ninety-day plan.

In my previous CEO positions, when I spoke with the board chair, vice chair, and other Executive Committee members who had been on the Search Committee that hired me, as well as other nonprofit executives that were partners and stakeholders, they inevitably asked, "How are things going for you?"

I always enjoyed answering this question. This gave me the perfect opening to describe the outcome of my meetings with staff and my observations. I took such opportunities to demonstrate the exhaustive research and skilled analysis that would drive decision-making throughout my leadership tenure.

During some conversations with external clients, I revisited questions the Search Committee asked me during its interview process. One question a board member posited to me before I was hired was, "How would you go about seeking funding from a foundation who used to support us but no longer does?"

Since first receiving that question, I learned a tremendous amount via my ninety-day goal. Soon after helming the nonprofit, I realized that the board member's inquiry was not speculative. Rather, the nonprofit had recently lost major funding from a foundation that had supported it for years. I now wanted to know the factors that resulted in losing its support.

Armed with real-world information about the nonprofit, I asked the board member nuanced questions for two reasons: first, so I could answer his initial question with more accuracy than before and, second, so I could gain more specific information that would improve my ability to solve the nonprofit's biggest challenges and better lead it. I followed up with him and the management team by asking the following questions:

- What details do you have about the foundation's original gift, including its history of giving to the nonprofit?
- When did the demise occur, including the date of the last gift?
- Did the foundation provide documentation that explains why we lost its support? Are there additional reasons why we lost its funding?
- Before I request a meeting with the foundation, who are the team or board members that could provide information regarding how the relationship fractured and why the funding was ultimately withheld?

Understanding the nonprofit's past, including its strengths, weaknesses, and good and bad decisions made, influences the direction I would take it in the future. I investigated how the nonprofit arrived where it was today, as well as the origins of the first level of support it received for specific programs. For example, the original funding might have started with a certain program, a capital project, or an initiative that directly supported a particular group of clients through disaster relief related to home fires, teen programs for girls, or CPR education and training.

In addition to the board, I spoke with anyone affiliated with the nonprofit who knew and appreciated its history and background. Through my conversations with people beyond the nonprofit staff, I learned how it gained funding from the donor, but the money was limited to some locations. In order to identify the strengths and weaknesses of the solicitation the nonprofit made to its donors, I investigated the reasons behind the organization's various levels of support.

My actions were to always seek to increase the donors' contributions and obtain as much unrestricted giving and funding as possible to meet the organization's needs. While my nonprofit always appreciated funding targeted to specific programs or locations, as CEO I also had to attract funding to cover the nonprofit's overhead and other important services. This is where honest and compelling conversations with current and potential supporters ultimately helped them understand the needs of the whole organization and not just its parts.

During one conversation, a board member told me the nonprofit did not perform well during an annual audit, why weaknesses weren't addressed prior to it, and where the organization needed to improve. Unfortunately, the rest of the board wasn't unaware of these significant problems. Thus I took the initiative to be the first to point these out to them.

In the case of conversations with nonprofit executives who were partners and stakeholders, the executives told me what they thought I should know now that I was the new leader.

The extensive meetings and tours I undertook created a ripple effect within the community my nonprofit served. Once word spread that I was hired and that my leadership was dramatically different from the CEO I replaced, people were curious to meet me. Professionals outside the groups I officially met with now took the initiative to schedule a time to meet with me. These included county and city employees who worked with my nonprofit, elected officials, past board chairs who were no longer on the board but wished to provide historical information about the organization's beginnings within the community, vendors who worked with us and had contacts that provided our nonprofit services such as insurance, health benefits, technology, and equipment, and vendors not currently working with our nonprofit but interested in offering their services.

In addition, national staff were assigned as the liaison to the local organization and worked with my team and me. These people had the role to debrief me and make sure I understood available resources from the national organization, how the organization I was operating ranked with similar budget-size organizations of other entities within the national federation of which the nonprofit belongs, and how my nonprofit was benchmarked within our peer group. They also provided other important national membership requirements to ensure our nonprofit met required standards. These national staff gave their perspective of how the organization performed under the prior administration and the changes they believed should be made. Rather than provide this information to me right away, these national staff waited a few months so I could focus on my new post. Afterwards, they began their checklist of items regarding reporting and other administrative requirements that had to be met.

Framework 1 brings you face-to-face with people in and outside the nonprofit in the most efficient and effective way possible. Once you meet your ninety-day goal, you have earned initial credibility as the new executive in charge.

Chapter 5

Framework 1: One-on-One Meetings during Your First Ninety Days

> **In this chapter, you'll learn:**
>
> - the essential information you need from your Human Resources (HR) Department during your first ninety days including:
>   - details about each department and employee prior to your one-on-one meetings with your direct reports in HR, Finance, Resource Development, Building and Maintenance, Program/Direct Service Delivery, and Communications and Marketing;
>   - specific benefits for employees prior to your meetings;
>   - three fundamental questions to ask about all departments;
> - key questions to ask your direct reports during your one-on-one meetings;
> - how to effectively assess and follow up with your direct reports after each meeting.

Your ninety-day plan demonstrates your two leadership personas. Both show you're a force for good for the nonprofit. First, the department meetings reflect that you, as the new CEO, are approachable, friendly, and a caring boss. This is your work family, and your initial meetings express your interest in your staff's well-being. Second, your one-on-one meetings drive home that you are disciplined, relentlessly committed to improvement, and determined to advance the nonprofit's mission.

In this chapter, we'll take a deep dive into the one-on-one meetings with your direct reports and the men and women outside your nonprofit that are key to accomplishing your ambitious professional goals. You'll discover a checklist comprising questions to ask your direct reports of the following departments: Human Resources, Finance, Resource Development, Building and Maintenance, Program/Direct Service Delivery, and Communications and Marketing.

While your organization may not have all departments listed, the questions in each checklist are applicable to all CEOs seeking to turn around troubled nonprofits or further strengthen and improve already thriving ones.

The objective of these questions is threefold: First, you are learning about your nonprofit. Second, you'll use the information you collect to guide future decisions you'll make. Third, once you complete these meetings, you'll identify the strengths and weaknesses of the nonprofit and its departments.

Internal Clients: Direct-Report, One-on-One Meetings

Prior to your meetings with your direct reports, you'll request your HR Department head to provide you with the job description and responsibilities for each position in every department and with a spreadsheet for each department with the following information for all employees within that department:

- Each person's name
- His or her title
- Full- or part-time status
- Demographic information such as gender, ethnicity, age, and highest degree completed
- Date of hire
- Years of service

I always request this information from the HR head my first week on the job because he or she may need time to put it together prior to meetings with department leaders. Sometimes the HR head doesn't directly report to me as CEO. In that case, I send my request to his or her supervisor as well.

You will study this information prior to your direct-report meetings and use it as a guide during each one-on-one appointment. As you review these fundamental details about your nonprofit, ask yourself, "What do these breakdowns tell me about each department?" For example, look for the experience level of the department as a whole and the individuals in it and how this may influence its strengths and weaknesses.

I also ask for the annual turnover rate of the entire nonprofit and each department over the last five years, which is a timeframe long enough to assess the organization's quality, as well as each team within it. High turnover warrants working with the department head to identify the causes behind this problem. Low turnover is a sign of team cohesion and prudent practices that may be worthwhile implementing in other departments.

One way to retain high-quality staff is through your benefits, which is why as CEO you need to understand your nonprofit's health insurance plans. You'll use them to keep current employees and as a selling point during your hiring efforts. While you're a nonprofit CEO and not the head of an insurance company, to fulfill your role effectively, you need to have basic knowledge of all your nonprofit's insurance policies.

Health Insurance: A Major Selling Point for Recruiting Top Employees

PRIOR TO YOUR ONE-ON-ONE department head meetings, request from the HR or Finance Department or both the employee health benefit guidelines that include employee health insurance plans. Staff, and specifically those with dependents, place a high priority on health insurance, along with a competitive salary among nonprofits. This is particularly the case in nonprofits where compensation tends to be lower than in the for-profit sector. Thus solid benefits such as health, dental, and vision insurance and vacation and sick days, along with retirement benefits for employees such as 401(k), IRA, or 403(b) plans can offset lower pay. When employers show prospective employees what they'll be earning annually by way of extensive benefits packages (these can appear as a benefits paycheck that shows the equivalent value of the benefits they earned beyond their base salary), these compensations beyond salary become a strong selling point. Also, because insurance is one of the largest expenses, CEOs need to have a grasp on this major budget item.

Part of effective leadership is having a general understanding of your organization's medical insurance plans, including copays. Along with the Finance and HR Departments, you should be part of the annual health insurance negotiation with providers and brokers, which means knowing health insurance basics.

In your hiring and recruiting role, you're charged to attract top talent in a highly competitive job market. If a major selling point of your nonprofit is your benefits, then making a compelling pitch to prospective employees requires knowledge about the benefits the organization provides. So research what the nonprofit currently offers and prepare questions you have about the health insurance offerings that you'll ask your HR Department leader.

Other Insurance: Obtain Information from HR and Finance Departments

IN ADDITION TO HEALTH INSURANCE, the following are other insurances to review: property, liability, casualty, vehicle, workers compensation, abuse and neglect, and director and officers, which covers the board of directors.

Such insurance coverages are imperative to manage risk, but their costs need to be scrutinized since all are big-budget items for most nonprofits. Obtain information from your HR or Finance

Department or both about your current plans. The type, cost, and amount of coverage you need depends on the direct services your organization provides and how many locations it has.

About four months before the current year ends on the coverage your organization has with providers, your nonprofit enters the annual insurance renewal period. During this time, you'll work with the HR and Finance Departments and insurance brokers. Representing the nonprofit, your broker obtains premium quotes and negotiates plans for the upcoming year.

When an organization is a part of a national federation, it has a set of minimum standards it suggests or requires for insurance coverage. In order to keep your nonprofit in compliance, you must know your national federation's guidelines.

For all insurances, if a board member has expertise, use it! Ask him or her to review insurance information with you and the Human Resources and Finance Departments before making a final recommendation. Next, keep your finance chair informed throughout the renewal period and regularly solicit his or her input. Also, insurance brokers are an educational resource and help you present these findings to your board for final approval for all insurance coverages.

In the next section, you'll learn the questions you'll direct to each department head. Seven business days is a reasonable timeframe to give them to provide their answers. But sometimes they'll need more time, particularly if they rely on their staff for certain replies. Request all answers to be submitted to you in written form at least twenty-four hours in advance of your one-on-one meeting. Let them know that during the appointment, you'll review the document together.

Human Resources Leader: Questions about the Entire Nonprofit

BEFORE THE MEETING, REVIEW THE SPREADSHEET the HR Department created for each department. Next, ask your HR direct report the following three questions about all departments:

- *How often are all-employee staff meetings held?*
  These are meetings you, as CEO, host with your direct reports. During these gatherings, departments describe what they're working on and future projects. They may also thank employees and other departments for their help completing previous projects or express their need for assistance in future ones. You direct this question to HR because HR is a neutral party that serves all departments and collects information about meetings. If regular all-staff and department meetings aren't held, then you need to inquire as to how information is shared and goals are achieved.
- *How often are department meetings held?*
  Rather than initially ask each direct report about its department meeting frequency, address this question first to HR, which will know this information due to employee feedback from exit interviews and annual evaluations of how departments are functioning. If it doesn't, then you may need to explore this with your HR leader.
- *What has been the format and focus of these department meetings?*
  During these meetings, departments evaluate their goals and objectives. For instance, the Finance Department

may discuss where it stands on closing the books. The Resource Development Department may assess its fundraising efforts. You want to know the frequency, substance, and quality of department meetings. Your job is to engage your staff and make sure they collaborate.

Human Resources Leader: Questions about the HR Department

- What are the strengths and weaknesses of the nonprofit's health and benefits package? From a hiring and recruiting perspective, how does it compare to other nonprofits?
- What special screenings, such as drug testing and background checks, need to be done specifically for staff, board members, and other volunteers within the organization? Do these special screenings take place for volunteers who may work with staff on various programs? (Each nonprofit has different policies regarding the background screening and drug testing of staff and volunteers. For its members, national organizations explicitly state their screening policy and expectations. For example, they may require volunteers who interact with clients on a regular basis to be screened like staff.)
- What do you think of the organization, board, and programs? Do you have other observations you want to share with me, as the CEO?
- What would you like to see continued, accomplished, or expanded?
- Do all staff meet the education-level requirements for each position?

- What is the annual budget for your department's staff?
- Does the nonprofit have an HR Committee? If yes, who leads it from the board level? If no, does another group such as the Executive Committee work with HR and the CEO? (All committees report to the board chair. All work is ultimately reported to the Executive Committee and board of directors. This is because within nonprofit bylaws both propose policies and eventually vote on what will be put into practice.)
- If the nonprofit has an HR Committee description, does it highlight the responsibilities of committee members and staff supporting the work?
- Have past or present employees filed any EEOC claims?
- Are any employees related to each other?
- Does the nonprofit have an official anti-nepotism policy?
- Does the nonprofit provide new staff an employee handbook that outlines all policies and guidelines?
- If so, does the nonprofit require employees to sign a document stating they have read and understand all the rules and policies in the employee handbook?
- When staff are hired, what is the orientation or training process or both they receive?
- Have employees or clients taken legal action against any departments regarding HR matters?
- Was or is the nonprofit subject to any sexual harassment, age discrimination, or other legal action brought about by employees, clients, or both?
- Over the last ten years, what have been the loss run reports for the nonprofit's insurance coverage? How have these affected insurance rates and premiums?

- What is the biggest settlement the nonprofit or its insurance company has had to pay as a result of any litigation? What are the details surrounding this settlement?
- What other settlements have been made by the organization and its insurance provider?
- Does the nonprofit work with an insurance broker to receive quotes from various providers on an annual basis?
- When is the nonprofit's open enrollment each year for health benefits?
- According to conversations you've had with department heads and employees, what do they like and not like about their health benefits?
- What are the nonprofit's policies regarding vacation, sick, and personal time?
- Over the last five years, what has been the history of pay or salary increases for the staff?
- Does every position within the organization have a job description? If yes, when was it last updated? If no, what is the reason behind the lack of job descriptions?

Chief Financial Officer or Financial Leader

BEFORE THE MEETING, REVIEW THE SPREADSHEET the HR Department created for the Finance Department. (In Framework 3, I'll present additional questions pertaining to activities of the Finance Department.)

- What do you think of the organization, board, and programs? Do you have other observations you want to share with me, as the CEO?
- What would you like to see continued, accomplished, or expanded?
- Do all staff meet the education-level requirements for each position?
- What is the annual budget for your department's staff?
- What are the monthly payroll requirements for the organization?
- How does the nonprofit process payroll?
- How are new hires processed and entered in the payroll system?
- How do the finance and HR departments work together to process payroll?
- Does the nonprofit have an electronic payroll system that employees use to track their time? If not, what is the manual payroll system and who oversees it?
- Does the nonprofit have standard operating procedures (SOPs) regarding payroll and other functions? If so, were these SOPs adopted by the board of directors? When was the last time these SOPs were reviewed and updated?
- How many board members make up the Finance Committee?
- How often do Finance Committee meetings take place?
- Does the finance chair or treasurer generate a report at every board meeting regarding the nonprofit's financial condition?

- What financial institution(s) does the nonprofit bank with? Is there more than one bank the nonprofit does business with? Why or why not?
- Are there any reasons, political, historical, or otherwise, regarding the selection of the financial institution the nonprofit uses to manage its money?
- If the nonprofit has an endowment, is there an investment policy and an investment committee that oversees it? How long has the nonprofit worked with the financial institution(s) regarding the investment of these funds?
- Who is responsible for developing the nonprofit's annual operating budget?
- What budget timeline does the nonprofit follow in order to develop its annual operating budget?
- Is the organization on a fiscal-year or calendar-year budget cycle? Is there a reason why one was chosen over the other?
- Is the nonprofit part of a federation or association? If so, what guidelines do we need to follow including benefits, insurance, and audits? Are we required to submit reports on an annual, quarterly, or monthly basis to the federation or association?

Resource Development Leader

BEFORE THE MEETING, REVIEW THE SPREADSHEET the HR Department created for the Resource Development Department. (In Framework 4, I'll present additional questions pertaining to activities of this department.)

- What do you think of the organization, board, and programs? Do you have other observations you want to share with me, as the CEO?
- What would you like to see continued, accomplished, or expanded?
- Do all staff meet the education-level requirements for each position?
- What is the annual budget for your department's staff?
- Have any of the resource development staff been with any other organization in a development capacity? If so, what fundraising experience, skill set, and talent do they bring to the department and nonprofit, and are these being effectively used?
- What are the greatest fundraising accomplishments of the department?
- How well does the resource development team understand the services that program staff deliver to clients? For example, have they observed staff providing these services?
- How does the Resource Development Department assess the programs, operating needs, and capital needs of each department? (Understanding these needs should play a role in the Resource Development Department's strategy to seek funding.)
- Does the nonprofit provide tours and other opportunities for donor, client, and staff engagement in order to build relationships and show the nonprofit's service-delivery activities?
- Are there other departments outside the Resource Development Department such as special events and planned and estate giving staff? (As CEO, you need to

understand all areas in which the organization is generating revenue. You also must have a firm grasp on how different departments share information, including if they have a process to provide potential leads to each other.)
- Does the nonprofit have Communications and Marketing staff, or are those responsibilities part of the development department?
- How many volunteers are actively part of the Resource Development Department?
- Does the nonprofit have a volunteer chair and committee who work with staff to seek funding from potential donors? (Volunteers can open doors for introductions of potential donors for the resource development staff and the CEO.)
- How are development goals established annually?
- Has there ever been an operating or capital needs campaign or both to expand the nonprofit's programs or services?

Building and Maintenance Leader

BEFORE THE MEETING, REVIEW THE SPREADSHEET the HR Department created for the Building and Maintenance Department.

- What do you think of the organization, board, and programs? Do you have other observations you want to share with me, as the CEO?

- What would you like to see continued, accomplished, or expanded?
- Do all staff meet the education-level requirements for each position?
- What is the annual budget for your department's staff?
- What is the department's annual budget for capital projects? Do not include janitorial or cleaning services.
- What have the capital expenditures been for the last five years? Do not include janitorial or cleaning services.
- Is the building and maintenance budget part of the annual operating budget, or is there a separate capital budget to track costs by location?
- When was the last time the insurance broker assessed these buildings for potential replacement value due to fire or Mother Nature?
- If not you, to whom does the department leader report on a daily basis?
- How many buildings or structures does the organization maintain on an annual basis?
- Is there a system to track when roofs, HVAC units, parking lots, sidewalks, and painting of buildings need to be replaced or refurbished? What other large-ticket items are in the capital budget?
- Do the Finance and Building and Maintenance Departments have a schedule of potential replacement project dates for capital items? What is the process under which these needs are communicated to the Resource Development Department for potential funding appeals?
- What is the process under which the Building and Maintenance Department communicates its needs to the resource development team?

- If the nonprofit has multiple locations, how many does it rent? How many does it own? Does it have a rolling five-year capital budget plan for building and maintenance costs by location? How much does insurance cost for each location?
- If the nonprofit rents facilities, what capital items is it responsible to maintain according to the lease?
- Does the nonprofit have agreements with local governments to use city, county, or state buildings to operate its programs?
- What are the policies that make sure the facility is safe for clients and staff?
- Does the nonprofit have capital budgets for each location to cover its annual work-requirement costs?

Program/Direct Service Delivery Leader

BEFORE THE MEETING, REVIEW THE SPREADSHEET HR created for the Program/Direct Service Delivery Department.

- What do you think of the organization, board, and programs? Do you have other observations you want to share with me, as the CEO?
- What would you like to see continued, accomplished, or expanded?
- Do all staff meet the education-level requirements for each position?
- What is the annual budget for your department's staff?

- Must each program maintain specific client-to-staff ratios? Please list those ratios for each program, along with any other important items for consideration regarding client services.
- How many people does each program serve on an annual basis?
- What is each program's operating budget for the last five years? (Show these expenses based on the fiscal year or calendar year reporting from your final audits because these will give actual results.)
- What electronic tracking system does the nonprofit use to verify and create reports of the number of clients served during any period?
- How many part- and full-time employees does each program have?
- What skill set does each program require staff to have to deliver services for each program?
- Does each program and program by location have a budget?
- How many programs currently operate within the organization?
- If the nonprofit has multiple locations, do all programs operate at each location? If no, why not?
- What revenues are restricted to certain programs? Do specific funding entities provide these restricted funds?
- How much unrestricted funding is used to support each program?
- Are there reimbursements for services for each or any of the nonprofit's programs?

- Are any program services supported by a reimbursement for services to your organization? (Reimbursement for services is a compensation model where the nonprofit only receives payment from the funder when the nonprofit provides documentation that services have been delivered. In other words, the nonprofit delivers the service upfront in good faith, anticipating receiving reimbursement in a timely manner. In later chapters, you'll see that invoicing these entities is important because it can affect cash flow. Government and quasi-government agencies follow this reimbursement structure.)
- What paperwork and billing must the nonprofit provide to receive the revenue from a funding entity?
- How long does receiving reimbursements from each funding sources take?
- What is the communication process program staff and the Finance Department use to ensure proper billing and receipting for all transactions? Is there a documented procedure that details the steps? If so, please provide this.
- How do clients qualify to receive services, and how is the success of the nonprofit's outreach and client-service delivery measured? (Your Communications and Marketing Department will use this information in its annual report and marketing materials.)
- How does the organization receive feedback from clients or the community regarding its service delivery?
- What type of annual training do part- and full-time staff undergo?
- What types of audits do funding sources perform? (For example, funding sources, such as local governments,

may contract third-party auditors to review an organization's financials, programs, staff qualifications, and more. And funding sources may make unannounced inspections where they measure the temperature of food the nonprofit serves to clients and evaluate the nonprofit's facilities and the programs it provides. Failing these stringent audits can result in a loss of funding. The Communications and Marketing and Resource Development Departments will use the credibility achieved in this way as a selling point to attract more funding sources.)

- What are the results of audits performed? In other words, what rating, scores, and strengths and weaknesses have they identified? (Similar to the point above, positive marks are a badge of honor and credibility. The Communications and Marketing and Resource Development Departments will use these results as selling points to attract more funding sources.)

Communications and Marketing Leader

BEFORE THE MEETING, REVIEW THE SPREADSHEET HR created for the Communications and Marketing Department.

- What do you think of the organization, board, and programs? Do you have other observations you want to share with me, as the CEO?
- What would you like to see continued, accomplished, or expanded?

- Do all staff meet the education-level requirements for each position?
- What is the annual budget for your department's staff?
- How does Communications and Marketing support the needs of the entire nonprofit and each of its departments?
- Does the nonprofit have a Communications and Marketing Committee that assists the staff in developing promotional marketing materials?
- Does the nonprofit have a communications and marketing plan?
- Does this department oversee all social media outreach on the organization's behalf? (If the community posts questions or comments on the nonprofit's social media accounts, the nonprofit should respond in a timely manner. Thus having a process and understanding regarding which department is responsible to reply to social media inquiries is key to effectively increasing community engagement.)
- Is this department responsible for keeping the organization's website and other social media platforms and public pages up-to-date? If yes, how is this done, and how does each department provide information to the Communications and Marketing Department? If no, who is in charge of these efforts, and what role does the Communications and Marketing Department play?
- Does this department oversee the creation of all marketing materials for the entire nonprofit and each of its departments?
- What is the nonprofit's protocol to address media inquiries? (In today's always-on social media age, a nonprofit must have a media policy that all staff follow. From

nonprofit crises to triumphs, its public communications responses should always be well planned and never improvised. For example, when the nonprofit receives a media inquiry, who is responsible to answer questions and how? Who is the first point of contact, and how does this person handle this initial inquiry? What are frequently asked questions and their standard replies?)
- For nonprofits part of a national organization: Does the national headquarters provide protocols and have compliance requirements for the nonprofit's branding or cause-related marketing campaigns or both? (If yes, review the protocols and the compliance requirements.)
- Does a marketing and advertising agency provide the nonprofit pro-bono services? (Given that nonprofits have limited to no marketing and advertising budgets, they especially benefit from pro-bono or deeply discounted services. Sometimes the company a board member represents works with an advertising agency and can request the agency help the nonprofit. If the answer is no, consider exploring if this is an option.)
- What have been the most challenging inquiries the media have made in the past? What were the weaknesses and strengths of the nonprofit's response?
- How does the Communications and Marketing Department obtain information from other departments regarding their accomplishments? (From four-star ratings from a third-party charity evaluation organization to a volunteer-of-the-year award, the Communications and Marketing Department must have a process by which it immediately receives information from other departments relevant to its marketing objectives.)

- How does the Communications and Marketing Department measure the success of its efforts to promote the organization?

Post One-on-One Meeting Follow-Up and Assessment

As you address the written responses to each question during your one-on-one meeting, your direct report's replies will change as a result of your time together. Think of the document your department head initially provided to you as a rough draft.

Together, you go through each question and answer in order to create a final draft. Some replies will stay the same, while others will change based on your discussion. For example, the direct report may have interpreted the question differently than you had intended, during the meeting you may have provided input that has changed or added more to the answer, or any number of circumstances can result in revised replies. Because you'll refer to this document later to make informed decisions for the nonprofit, you want the clearest version possible for your records.

"You answered all my questions and we made some changes, so please send an updated version back to me," you tell your direct report.

Then after the meeting, he or she will prepare a final draft that addresses the revisions you both made to the document.

Once you've completed several interviews, you'll be able to identify commonalities and differences between department responses. One of the most significant benefits of these meetings is the information they provide that allows you to assess each department and the entire nonprofit.

In particular, the initial questions ("What do you think of the organization, board, and programs? Do you have any other observations you want to share with me, as the CEO?" and "What would you like to see continued, accomplished, or expanded?") provide important insight that you can use to compare departments to each other. Certain answers may elicit similar replies between departments, while others may be outliers. Alignment of work ethic, values, and mission between departments and volunteers is a good sign. But if you identify misalignment and other weaknesses, you will then do the work of figuring out underlying problems you need to fix. Now that you've learned how to address your internal clients, in the next chapter you'll learn about your external clients.

Chapter 6

Framework 1: The Three Ts and Measuring Performance during Your First Ninety Days

> **In this chapter, you'll learn:**
> - the importance of the Three Ts—time, talent, and treasure—and how they influence the actions and thoughts of everyone connected with your nonprofit;
> - how the financial giving and attendance scorecards will provide your nonprofit remarkable long-term benefits;
> - the value of the Three Gs—give, get, and go—and how to apply them in assessing the quality of your board members.

LAURA WAS A BOARD MEMBER of a nonprofit I was leading. She described to me a conversation she had with Steve, a successful entrepreneur in her vast network. In addition to his business acumen, Steve was also well-known for his philanthropy.

"I was always taught you give till it hurts," Laura told him.

"Really? I was taught the opposite: You give till you feel really good!" Steve said.

She appreciated his positive spin on her somewhat negative perspective on giving. Steve not only changed her opinion, but his words also influenced how she would approach giving when reaching out to other contacts in her network.

Our nonprofit benefitted immensely from Laura's connection to Steve and his unflagging optimism and perspective on giving back. In fact, Steve both donated generously and opened doors for us to connect with other equally successful and generous men and women in his network.

Giving until it feels really good is also a leadership philosophy. As CEO, you're heading an organization that emphasizes the role those outside your nonprofit play in improving their communities and the lives of those within in it. Your donors' **treasure** (in other words, their financial contribution) is the significant and meaningful gift to your nonprofit and is one of the Three Ts.

Time, Talent, and **Treasure** summarize how people and organizations give to your nonprofit. The Three Ts form the foundation of your leadership strategy when it comes to the groups of people you'll meet outside your nonprofit staff, including philanthropists like Steve. Your three donor classes are as follows:

1. Board of directors
2. Individual donors
3. Corporate and foundation supporters

Specifically, when it comes to your first ninety days, you'll use the Three Ts as a guide to meet with your top donors within each of these three donor groups. The Three Ts will drive how you strengthen your network, build your board, train your staff, and grow your nonprofit. In the following section, we'll explore each T.

Time

ACCORDING TO THE CORPORATION for National and Community Service, more than seventy-seven million Americans, or 30 percent of adults, volunteer their time to making a difference. Of the 1.54 million charitable organizations in the United States, your volunteers have chosen to allocate their time to your organization at the sacrifice of countless other activities. Through your nonprofit, they are pledging their time to make a difference in their communities.

Throughout my career leading nonprofits, I've always sought to know what motivated people to join and support our organization.

I ask, "Have you, your families, or someone else close to you been served by our nonprofit?"

Yes is a frequent reply. They'll then often explain how the nonprofit met a deep need for them or someone they cared about.

A no response often means that, even though the nonprofit hasn't touched their lives directly, they have a passion and compassion for the mission. Without a prior connection to the nonprofit, they might have researched it. As a result, they've gained respect for its mission and positive work within the community. Other reasons people volunteer are to broaden their network, learn about their communities in a way only possible through helping fulfill the nonprofit's mission, develop new friendships, generate new business contacts, and surround themselves with likeminded people who seek to make a difference.

I also had the good fortune of working with community leaders who sought to have their up-and-coming executives within their companies experience the importance of supporting the community through nonprofit service. By volunteering their time, they would use their expertise to improve an organization outside their own company, expand their skills and experience, and learn about their community.

If an employee's boss places a high priority on supporting your nonprofit, then this focus becomes important to the professional who has been asked to serve. In addition, companies use their employees' volunteer work to recognize and reward them, and companies gain firsthand knowledge of the nonprofits to which they've pledged their time and money.

This refers to the gift of skill, intellectual property, and networking that people in the three groups share with the nonprofit. In order to turn around a struggling nonprofit or grow a thriving one, you must understand the type of talent it needs. From there, you'll recruit individuals with the specific skill sets that fill in talent gaps within your organization. The talent you bring in must make your organization stronger. This points to the importance of nominating committees: As you recruit new board members, you are looking for the women and men who will lead your nonprofit into the future.

As CEO, you will work in tandem with your board chair, Nominating Committee chair, and members of the committee to identify the talent you need to change and enhance your nonprofit. During the Nominating Committee process, you'll assess the professions and people represented on the current board. If the roster is dominated by a particular business or industry, you'll go about identifying what other businesses, including startups, would improve your board. You'll consider a person's expertise, perspective, experience, social and business contacts, wisdom, gender, ethnicity, age, and socioeconomic status.

For example, entrepreneurs have a different skill set than corporate executives. Having both mindsets on the board would bring about diverse and powerful perspectives.

Once you've determined the profile of board members your nonprofit will benefit from, consider reaching out to your individual, corporate, and foundation donors for references of people who can serve as potential board members.

Treasure

THERE'S NO DOUBT ABOUT IT, Americans love to give. People are more likely to donate their treasure if, while growing up, their parents modeled philanthropy. In 2021, 56 percent of US adults donated to charitable organizations with their contributions totaling a whopping $326 billion. In addition to individual contributions, in 2021 corporations gave $21 billion and foundations $90 billion. *Treasure* refers to the financial contribution your board members and individual, corporate, and foundation donors make to your nonprofit.

These significant and meaningful financial gifts are prerequisites for board membership and ones your nonprofit will always explicitly express gratitude for. To find treasure as a CEO, you must actively seek it. You must be bold, creative, assertive, and excited about your nonprofit's mission.

In general, it's far more cost effective and time efficient to keep current donors than to find new ones. In addition to retaining your present donors, you also want to find ways to increase their annual contributions. While maintaining and strengthening your relationships with your roster of donors, you're also charged to attract new ones by continually cultivating connections.

A common truism in our industry is that **PEOPLE GIVE TO PEOPLE, NOT NONPROFITS.** To meet this aim as CEO, you're responsible to create meaningful and lasting connections with people in your community. You'll also assess your board's and staff's abilities to do this and provide training and mentoring if they require additional support.

In addition, your board members are responsible to raise money for the nonprofit through reaching out to those within their network that have the capacity to give. Your board members represent companies that may have both corporate resources to support your nonprofit's mission and a corporate foundation. In this instance, inquire about the application process to qualify for foundation support. Or board members may have connections through their professional and personal networks to other granting organizations such as private or family foundations or both.

In fact, people at the company your board member represents may be waiting for him or her to make a financial appeal. When it comes to foundations and granting organizations, some may require details about your board members' financial contributions. For example, through their application process, some granting organizations ask if 100 percent of a nonprofit's board members are donating money. If it is yes, they may even ask for the average level of giving or what the board committed as a whole the prior year. Keep in mind you should never disclose individual giving amounts because this information is confidential unless the donor explicitly granted consent.

Now, let's take a deep dive into the one-on-one meetings with the men and women you will have outside your nonprofit that are key to accomplishing your ambitious professional goals.

Board of Directors: Prior to Your Meeting

One-on-One Meetings outside Your Nonprofit: Research Prior to Your Meetings

JUST AS HEAD COACHES NEED THE best players on their teams from day one on the job, you need top talent on your board from the start to ensure a winning inaugural season. First, you must assess your nonprofit's roster and see what board of director positions you need to fill.

Fortunately, before you've even begun your ninety days, you know some players on your bench—you've already met board members during the search-committee process. In addition, through your prior leadership positions and vast network, you may have connections to current board members, who will be also referred to as **volunteers** throughout this chapter. You'll use this information to evaluate your board's quality.

Next, identify who records meeting minutes and attendance for your nonprofit's board and Executive Committee meetings. This person is usually your executive assistant who provided minutes to the prior CEO for review and approval. At the next board meeting, the members took an official vote to approve the minutes from the previous meeting as recorded. Depending on how long your executive assistant has served in this capacity, he or she will help you complete the **board scorecard**.

What Are Board Scorecards?

A STRONG BOARD DIRECTLY TRANSLATES TO a significant boost of unrivaled time, talent, and treasure for the nonprofit via each volunteer's participation. Thus during my initial recruitment interviews with Search Committees prior to my eventual appointment as CEO, I asked the following question when we broached the subject of the nonprofit's board of directors:

"What is your process to hold present board members accountable and recruit ideal future volunteers?"

With each nonprofit I interviewed with, I received a variation on the following reply:

"Some board members perform well and fully participate, while others need to step up to make our nonprofit even stronger. Unfortunately, we don't have a process to maintain high outcomes across the entire current board or to recruit ideal future volunteers."

Through my experience, I saw that while most board members worked to meet the organization's needs, many nonprofits struggled to have all board members fulfill their individual Three-T pledges. In addition, improving performance and participation was a delicate topic, given that board engagement was voluntary.

Next, without a quantifiable and consistent way to measure each board member's engagement level, any volunteer-recruiting process lacked effective focus to bring on ideal candidates that would fill specific needs within the board. The board, CEO, and nominating committee will use the nonprofit's strategic plan (which has identified its future needs) as a guide to determine the type of prospective board members that will best further the nonprofit's mission. For example, the expertise of CPAs and other financial professionals will benefit the Finance Committee. In addition, these financial specialists, plus bankers and lawyers, can improve how the nonprofit addresses endowment and estate giving, trusts, and other donor-advised funds. Communications professionals can work with the Communications and Marketing Committee to improve how the nonprofit reinforces its brand and promotes itself within the community. Professionals from the construction and building trades can analyze facilities and consult on requests for proposals (RFPs) regarding building and renovation projects. If a nonprofit lags when it comes to web development and computer hardware and software infrastructure, board members with IT expertise such as entrepreneurs who are part of tech startups can guide nonprofits toward making prudent decisions amid the countless and costly technology options available.

Throughout the nonprofit industry, I've seen that organizations without a clearly and fully developed strategy to solve its biggest challenges as outlined in their strategic plans welcome CEOs who know how to improve board performance. Thus, after being hired, I always placed top priority on boosting board accountability and engagement. To do so requires a thorough assessment of the board's strengths and weaknesses. As I thought about how to increase participation and performance, I was reminded of the saying "What gets measured gets done."

The first step to improving the board was to have an objective performance and participation metric. Second, the strategy I developed needed to earn the credibility and thus the engagement of the board chair and the Nominating Committee.

To address the first step, I developed the **board scorecards** and gave myself a deadline of two months after the start of my tenure to analyze their results. There are two scorecards: **attendance** and **financial giving**. Together they cover the Three Ts.

Time and talent (via attendance) and treasure (via financial giving) are the lifeblood of a nonprofit's ability to fulfill its mission. With these two scorecards tracked over two years, I quickly see who is engaged with my nonprofit. These men and women give at higher levels, attend board meetings, and provide their expertise, thus meeting their commitment to be an effective board member.

The two scorecards became the starting point and centerpiece of my strategy to establish a standard of board excellence in partnership with the board. The remarkable results that came from them are why I recommend you create them too.

In order to effectively evaluate your board's quality, your nonprofit needs an empirical process to assess the performance and participation of each board member. Just as with the annual performance reviews I conducted with employees, the scorecards are designed to make objective decisions and to facilitate conversations regarding board member performance.

The scorecard results are part of the Nominating Committee's annual review process. Rather than provide my opinion about the scores of each board member, as CEO, my role is to provide factual data for review. The results of the scorecards speak for themselves. It removes me, as CEO, from having to play bad cop. In addition, as CEO, I walk a fine line when it comes to board appointments. I am in charge of hiring staff. Meanwhile, the Nominating Committee—not me—is responsible for bringing on new membership. But I cannot meet my ambitious goals for the nonprofit without the board's backing, expertise, and support. Thus our interests should align. To strike the balance between influencing the board member selection process and keeping proper distance from direct decisions about appointments, I work in partnership with the volunteers. The scorecard is the most effective way for me to maintain proper boundaries and avoid stepping out of my assigned duties.

Once the four spreadsheets are created for the financial giving and attendance for the current and past fiscal years, I now have a comprehensive performance and attendance data when the Nominating Committee reviews the current board's effectiveness.

With the board scorecard, the Nominating Committee does not look to me to evaluate board members and point out those who aren't meeting their commitments. Rather, the objective information is self-evident. I implement and execute the scorecard and show the findings to the board chair and Nominating Committee so they can evaluate board members and draw their own conclusions.

To keep the board scorecards as straightforward and effective as possible, I narrow the grading criteria to two categories, each recorded in a separate spreadsheet: financial giving and attendance. This information is then completed for the immediately preceding and current fiscal years for a combined total of four scorecards reflected in four spreadsheets.

The Financial Giving Scorecard and the Three Gs

To begin creating the financial giving scorecard, I appoint my executive assistant to prepare the headers for each document that I pass on to other staff to complete and review where appropriate.

For each of the two fiscal years, there is a separate financial giving spreadsheet with the following columns with one line completed for each board member:

1. Board member's last name, all listed in alphabetical order
2. Board member's first name
3. Company the board member works for
4. Board member's personal giving
5. Board member's corporate giving
6. Board member's foundation giving
7. Total board member's personal, corporate, and foundation giving
8. Comments and details

The last line on the spreadsheet shows the total for each of the four giving columns (4, 5, 6, and 7 above). My CFO inputs the financial giving amounts on each of the two spreadsheets based on the last two fiscal year donations. With data entered, I then send the financial spreadsheet to the Resource Development Department where its officer and team verify dollar amounts and add comments, which are always short. They highlight any specific purpose of gifts for quick reference by those reviewing the scorecard. We can see which gifts were unrestricted (always our preference) and which were tied to a stated intent. Comment examples are "co-chaired 100 Women event," "corporate donation for golf tournament secured by board member," and "foundation gift for capital campaign"—all of which were restricted gifts but nonetheless meaningful to our work.

Many aspects of my role as CEO are divided between the head and the heart. I'm charged to set goals, hold myself and my team accountable, and produce measurable results—this illustrates the head.

In order to meet my objectives, I'm responsible to work well with and motivate my staff, board, and community members. To do so requires interpersonal, negotiation, and communication skills, which are all part of having high emotional intelligence—this illustrates the heart.

Effective leadership requires both head and heart to work together. The financial scorecard is an example of the head. Let's now see how appealing to the heart makes it a must-have resource, one that has the power to transform your board into the most effective in the history of your nonprofit.

At the start of a board meeting during my tenure with one of my nonprofits, I invited Tommy to speak. While only seventeen years old, he was mature far beyond his years and pushed to grow up even faster by his difficult life circumstances.

"If it weren't for this organization, I would have become a victim of the streets . . . I know this because many of the kids growing up in my neighborhood wound up in gangs, on drugs, and worse," he said.

Tommy had been a member of the nonprofit since he was seven years old. At the time, he was being raised by his mom and didn't know his dad. Over the next decade, our nonprofit became his second home. He arrived to our organization after school where he made friends and was surrounded by responsible grownups. In particular, the organization provided him positive, upstanding male role models in his life that he otherwise wouldn't have had.

As the years progressed, the little boy became the man of the house. His mom's health deteriorated to the point where she was often bedridden and required dialysis twice a week. His younger brother had autism and needed Tommy's constant care when they were at home. Every morning, he helped his disabled mom and brother prepare for the day, which included dressing them and making breakfast. Despite the burden he carried, Tommy was an honor roll student and always helped in the nonprofit. In fact, when he was old enough, he became a youth worker, which meant running programs and earning income. For a responsible kid like Tommy, the financial compensation provided both a reward and an incentive to continue working hard.

As he set his sight on the future, Tommy was excited to attend college. With no role models in his immediate family to rely on, he received the needed guidance and support from the staff as he transitioned into his next life stage, which included entrance and loan applications. With a degree, he would be the first college graduate in his family.

"The organization got me through countless hard times, and I wouldn't have been able to make it this far without everyone's support," he said.

After the young man gave his short talk, the board gave him a heartfelt round of applause. Some were moved to tears while others had bright smiles on their faces. They were all proud of Tommy and the nonprofit.

I start every board meeting with a **mission moment**, which is when I invite a guest like Tommy to give a brief account of how the nonprofit met a major need and improved his or her life. When I headed another nonprofit, I recall a guest speaker describing how she lost everything after a devastating natural disaster and was grateful for the safety, resources, and shelter our organization provided her and her family during their greatest time of need.

To serve on a board requires a special type of person. Meeting the obligations of the Three Ts is not easy. The best volunteers are driven by compassion, a deep desire to benefit their communities, and a willingness to use their skills to improve the nonprofit. In other words, they are abundantly volunteering their time and talent. Then there's the giving of their treasure by way of their financial pledge. The hard work board members perform—planning fundraising events, donating and raising money, evaluating RFPs and contracts, poring over legal documents and spreadsheets, and more—is critical to the nonprofit's success but often removed from directly serving clients. The mission moments connect the vital work that volunteers perform to those benefitting from their dedication and service. The stories are intended to inspire your board members to become engaged with the nonprofit they represent. With the big challenges nonprofits face, the work is tough. As CEO, I had my share of long and completely draining days where I knew I needed to be reenergized. When I was feeling depleted, I made an effort to visit a facility and see how my staff was putting smiles on clients' faces, getting them through rough times in their lives, and providing them essential resources they otherwise wouldn't have received. Afterward, I always came back energized, realizing the stress I carried served an incredible purpose.

Similarly, mission moments provide emotional nourishment and generate passion for your board. Mission moments delivered well have motivated my board members to do what I did after the end of a tough work day. They sought further inspiration by walking through our facilities and chatting with clients and staff. I always knew the work our nonprofit did was fulfilling to see in action, so when board members wanted to visit our operations, I welcomed their enthusiasm and presence. Witnessing with their own eyes the incredible work taking place brought the mission alive to them. They observed the fruits of their volunteer participation, as well as the challenges our organization faced.

One of the most significant strengths of the board scorecard is it quantifies whether board members have met their financial commitments. If the nonprofit does not compare the actual performance of each board member to his or her stated goals, then the financial benchmarks are weak if not meaningless. The scorecard measures the amount of dollars each board member has raised. This definitive assessment is part of a nonprofit's **Three G** approach, which requires all board members to accept an individual fundraising goal annually as a part of their board commitment.

The first G is internal and the second is external. Board members will **give** at the highest individual level they can afford—this is the internal part. Or they will **get** their friends, acquaintances, peers, and organizations they have a relationship with to contribute—this is the external part. Or they will combine both internal and external to meet their financial pledge. If they are unwilling or unable to fulfill the first two Gs, then they may be asked to **go** from the board.

The advantage of following the Three Gs is twofold. First, you attract motivated board members who are confident they will serve to benefit the nonprofit in the most tangible way possible: through their treasure. Second, it shows donors that your nonprofit is competitive and has high expectations by setting goals for its board members, which also lends credibility to the nonprofit and your leadership of it.

Regarding the third G, I left it out of my conversations with volunteers. The scorecards were the foundation of my strategy to build a great board, and the first two Gs aligned with the data reflected in them. They provided us the information required to have an objective conversation about poor or exceptional performance. Focusing on the two Gs reflected my leadership approach, which was positive, inspiring, and evidence based. With leaders within my nonprofit, we spoke about the Three Gs in regard to board member duties. Even in these instances, we paid moderate attention to the third G. We found our focus would be better spent training and providing our volunteers' resources on how to meet the first two Gs. No board members would be forced to go strictly because they didn't meet a financial commitment. This points to another strength of having two scorecards. Underperformance in one scorecard could be offset by high performance in another. But if both scorecards ranked low, then there was a need to have a conversation with the volunteer regarding performance.

With solid support and guidance for volunteers who had drifted off track, they often wound up meeting their goals. Also, striking a positive tone with board members is critical to encourage them to perform at their best in their volunteer capacity. Ultimately, my volunteers would know if they needed to pull the trigger on the third G. Only when good-faith efforts were not made to achieve their individual goals after we had had a clear conversation regarding the lack of performance were they asked to go. This happened so infrequently that we deemed bringing up the third G unnecessary and needlessly punitive. In most cases, if someone was not performing well, the person usually would step aside on his or her own after acknowledging not meeting the objectives.

This points to the role of the financial scorecard in creating the best board possible. The scorecard is meaningful only if it results in volunteers meeting their targets. Establishing measurable benchmarks for board members is a fundamental step to set them up to succeed in their volunteer capacity. But scorecards alone are cold, callous, and incomplete. Agreeing upon give and get amounts and then measuring them are easy in comparison to the support nonprofits provide to their volunteers to meet their financial objectives.

During my first ninety days at all the nonprofits I worked for, board members had pledged individual annual give and get amounts. These could be thousands or tens of thousands of dollars, depending upon the give and get goals established by board leadership. In one nonprofit I served, it was a ten-thousand-dollar goal per person per year for the give and get. While nonprofits setting give and get amounts is prudent, the problem I saw was weak to nonexistent follow-up to hold board members accountable.

The **mission moments** regularly reminded board members how the money they raised was directly improving clients' lives. I find that the more board members are shown how much their work is strengthening the most vulnerable among us, the more effort they put forth. When they see the big problems the nonprofit is tackling in its community, they want to be part of the solution.

While some volunteers met their **give** commitment on their own, I found that many relied, sometimes extensively, on their **get** channel. Even board members who cut personal checks every year to meet their pledge (thereby carrying out their **give** commitment) benefitted from strengthening their **get** skills.

A board member may have experience raising money or soliciting it. For instance, salespeople and entrepreneurs who generate clients and funding for their companies have developed a skill set that facilitates raising money on behalf of the nonprofit. But other board members may not have this background, and they're looking to you for help.

In my experience working with multiple boards, I have come to some conclusions. First, people don't like raising money. Second, people hate rejection. Considering that raising money requires rejection and the more you raise, the more you'll expose yourself to noes, this presents a tough challenge to nonprofits.

Here's where your leadership can result in tapping into fundraising potential that would otherwise go unnoticed. Building a team of fundraisers via your board members requires extensive training, resources, and support. You are giving your volunteers a formula and strategy to grow into their role as inspiring and influential ambassadors on behalf of your organization. Just as effective onboarding procedures and employee orientation set your internal team up for success, similar practices help your board members build the confidence and skills they need to serve effectively. In fact, during all board orientations, I described the scorecards. Part of setting volunteers up for success is to clearly outline what they're expected to do, including meeting their give and get goals. And during the nominating process prior to the orientation, we provide prospective board members a document that outlines volunteer roles and responsibilities, including Three T commitments. Once people know what their obligations are, they'll remove themselves from the nominating process early on if they feel they won't be able to meet those expectations. Or, if they agree to join the board and are selected, they'll then plan how they'll meet their financial pledge. Modeling and upholding clear communication are woven into every process you spearhead as CEO.

Key to raising money effectively is having an abundance mindset, which means you know that treasure is out there. Thus a volunteer's job is to be a treasure hunter. This is the opposite of a scarcity mindset that believes in limited opportunities that seem to shrink over time. Board members can solicit donations through pledge drives, sponsor tables at a gala, offer products or services for auction at a fundraising dinner, purchase auction items, sell tickets for an event, invite guests that will donate at a fundraiser, or receive a commitment from a gala attendee to provide matching funds during a donation appeal at the event itself. This abundance list is limitless.

At a board meeting after an event, my board chair and I always enjoyed proudly recognizing volunteers for their achievements:

"I'm sincerely thankful that Barbara's company purchased a table for $2,500. And one of her guests purchased a $1,500 wine-tasting weekend that was up for auction!"

Or:

"I'm so thankful that for this year's live auction Stan's company donated two tickets to its suite for every event that takes place at the arena next year. We know his company has requested that we accept a ten-thousand-dollar minimum donation for these two tickets to the luxury box as the value is far beyond that amount, and we'll surely stick to that!"

Your resource development staff will provide your volunteers expertise to support their fundraising. One way for them to improve their skills is to have them participate in an Event Committee. Every event has one, and your resource development staff will work with volunteers to make the event as successful as possible. Through their participation, they'll improve their fundraising ability. In addition, board members with fundraising prowess can serve as coaches. They can teach new volunteers their effective give and get strategies.

As a CEO, you set the tone. When you're able to express your enthusiasm for the tremendous role your nonprofit plays in the community, your energy is infectious. I found volunteers so excited to fulfill their duties that they told me, "Brian, I don't want to raise only ten thousand dollars. I want to go *way* past that. Let's do this!" When I heard such motivated voices, I took it as evidence of a job well done on my part encouraging my board. Now, I was prepared to do whatever I could to support them in their zeal to exceed their obligations. In order to ride this wave of eagerness and to help those who were struggling, I was responsible to guide them.

The Attendance Scorecard Is a Reflection of Time and Talent

WHEN YOUR BOARD COMPRISES VOLUNTEERS with talents that meet specific needs you've identified and they allocate an admirable amount of time filling these voids, you know you have built a dream team. Volunteers dedicating their time and talents to your nonprofit to their highest ability is an unstoppable force for producing amazing results. While your volunteers' presence in board meetings in and of itself doesn't equate to peak performance, it is the foundation for their being fully engaged with the nonprofit. Thus their presence is required. This is the rationale behind the attendance scorecard.

For the attendance spreadsheet, I have my assistant input the immediately preceding fiscal year with board members' full names, listed alphabetically by last name. My EA then inputs the attendance record information on the spreadsheet based on participation recorded in previous board minutes.

During your onboarding process, you'll clearly outline the responsibilities of board members, including their attendance requirements. An effective board orientation meeting shows volunteers that your nonprofit places a high priority on each board member's contribution of time and talent—your nonprofit, which includes its board, takes its mission seriously.

In one nonprofit I headed, only two absences were allowed per year, and we asked volunteers to notify us if they wouldn't be able to attend a meeting. From September through June, the nonprofit held ten meetings. As a newly appointed CEO, I looked at the scorecard to identify attendance trends, strengths, and weaknesses.

The scorecard holds volunteers accountable for short- and long-term attendance. I have my EA update it on an ongoing basis to track meeting-to-meeting participation, as well as for the entire year. That way, I'm able to spot absences early so I can address any issues quickly in order to increase participation. Thus the scorecard serves the purpose of evaluating volunteer performance for the entire year and solving poor attendance early on.

When volunteers know their role is important, their presence is appreciated, their time is valued, and their attendance is tracked, I have consistently seen poor attendance improve and solid participation stay that way. Improving participation requires striking the balance between sending the message to volunteers that "we're watching you" and reminding yourself they're volunteers with no obligation other than their personal pledge to stick with the nonprofit. Being aware of the latter means critiques will discourage rather than encourage them. People often have legitimate reasons why they're not participating, so keep this in mind as you determine the best way to increase volunteer participation.

The Naughty and Nice List: Using Scorecards to Improve Underperformance and Reward High Achievement

ONCE YOU'VE GENERATED YOUR TWO SCORECARDS tracked over two years, you've poured a strong foundation to increase volunteer performance. Without your scorecards, any measures you take to increase accountability are like building a house on sandy soil. But with your scorecards, you have done the hard work that will ensure the next steps you'll take are set on solid ground.

After reviewing them, I present the completed scorecards to relevant parties. As CEO, my duty is to work with my board chair to establish a standard of excellence for engagement. In order to accomplish this task, at the beginning of my leadership tenure, I pitch the scorecards effectively to the chair to gain his or her support. To meet this objective, I provide background about the scorecards' development and describe how previous nonprofits I served lacked a process to improve volunteer underperformance. I explain how I sought to hold the nonprofit and the board members accountable. My strategy to solve these problems started with the scorecards.

Board chairs always appreciate my backstory and understand the role the scorecards play. Through my explanation, they see the lengths I've gone through to advance the organization's mission. They appreciate my ability to innovate and drive to do what is best for the nonprofit.

Next, I always keep the scorecards confidential because they contain personal information about each board member. I make sure only my board chair, Nominating Committee, and I have access to them. During meetings with the Nominating Committee and board chair, I provide hard copies of scores to meeting participants, let them know they are confidential, and then collect the documents at the end of our time together.

My first round of review is with the board chair. During our meeting, I receive his or her preliminary assessment of the board based on the scorecard, including thoughts, reactions, and performance of each volunteer. For example, let's say the spreadsheet records ten board meetings. We quickly see those volunteers who have 100 percent attendance and those who have one or two absences. While personal and professional circumstances can result in missing a couple of meetings, if many board members aren't hitting the 80 percent mark, their collective lack of contributing time will hurt the nonprofit. Or we identify members who aren't meeting their give and get commitments. Or we note which volunteers deserve public praise for meeting or exceeding their Three T pledge. In the next chapter, you'll learn how I address various scenarios of board performance.

Chapter 7

Framework 1: Communication Protocols during Your First Ninety Days

> **In this chapter, you'll learn:**
>
> - how to establish amazing and lasting relationships with your volunteers;
> - effective approaches to addressing underperforming volunteers;
> - powerful strategies to prepare for interviews with your executive assistant and staff;
> - key questions to answer prior to one-on-one meetings with your chair, individual volunteers and donors, and corporate and foundation sponsors;
> - the five steps to effective meetings;
> - essential questions to ask your contributors.

BY SPOTTING AND SKILLFULLY ADDRESSING VOLUNTEER underachievement early, financial giving or attendance or both may improve. The financial giving and attendance scorecards point out board members who have exceeded their Three

T commitments, as well as those who have gone astray. When underperforming board members are provided resources and support, rather than resign, they often step up and meet their obligations. Identifying volunteer issues early facilitates conversations with struggling volunteers that would otherwise not take place and improves overall communication.

Phone calls and informal meetings create stronger connections between volunteers. When it comes to who is responsible to communicate directly with underperforming volunteers, I usually defer these delicate and essential conversations to the following individuals in order of frequency:

- The board chair
- A person on the nominating committee who chooses to take this on as his or her responsibility
- The individual who initially nominated the underperforming volunteer
- The CEO

Board chairs are well qualified to make these calls because they're leaders and as such they are acting on behalf of the board and the nonprofit. In addition, taking on this role can be part of their leadership responsibility. People on the nominating committee are well qualified because of their connection to all present volunteers from their participation in the past selection process. People who initially nominated the person are well suited because of the personal connection they have with the individual.

In the event the board chair and I agree that my participation is the best approach, I'll make the call. But this is the exception rather than the norm. Because these volunteers are my bosses, I stay out of these conversations. Whenever possible, I avoid being seen as the bad guy or heavy. Thus, unless we deem my involvement will increase the likelihood of the improvement we seek, I defer these conversations to the other three individuals. Furthermore, because volunteers nominate and vote on fellow volunteers who will serve on the board, as well as dismiss them for underperformance, I leave these difficult conversations to volunteers to have among themselves. While I provide my opinion when asked, I leave performance and attendance talks to volunteers. In fact, I have had board members explicitly tell me, "Brian, no CEO should be put in that place of addressing issues with volunteers. That's our job, not yours." While my scorecard results in flagging volunteers who aren't meeting their commitments and without it underachievement may go unnoticed, I leave taking action to the board chair or the assigned person willing to make the call.

On occasion volunteers contact me directly to explain their current circumstances when they know they have not been fulfilling their commitment.

"Brian, I'm really going through the ringer right now. I definitely want to stay on the board. I just need some time. How do I do it?" When I deem it appropriate, I respond, "If you would like, I can have a talk with the board chair, and from there, we can determine our options." This is another example of a conscientious board member who could turn into a loyal and strong volunteer once his or her life turns around for the better.

Keep in mind low scores in any area are not intended to shame or embarrass. Rather, they indicate which board members have met their obligations and how to communicate with those who haven't. In the next section, you'll learn three common scenarios I've encountered in regard to a volunteer's Three Ts.

Overachieving Volunteers: Three Ts to a Tee

AT ONE NONPROFIT, THE BOARD CHAIR and I reviewed a particular board member's scores. We compared Jeff's personal, corporate, and foundation financial contributions to his give and get goals. According to Jeff's results, he helped us raise nearly three hundred thousand dollars in one fiscal year; he was a dream board member! Such generosity is exceptional, and it reflects the importance of calculating and reviewing all three categories of giving. According to his attendance, he missed only one out of ten board meetings, and the by-laws allowed for two absences. I remember presenting Jeff's scores to my board chair. While we all knew Jeff was a great volunteer, even the chair was surprised to see his outstanding performance. "I guess I need to give him another call to thank him and his company for everything they have done this year!" the chair told me.

Absentee Volunteers: Less Talent and Time and Sometimes More Treasure

IMAGINE ONE NONPROFIT'S ATTENDANCE RECORD SHOWS Alex has both crossed the two-absence maximum in its by-laws and never let the board chair or CEO know in advance that he wouldn't attend after the requests for RSVPs for each meeting were sent to board members. Meanwhile, he's been on target with his giving. The board chair and CEO speak about how to best address Alex's absences with him. Robin and the CEO decide the prudent approach is for her to give Alex a friendly, informal phone call.

In a non-accusatory way, during their conversation, Robin asks, "Just checking in, Alex. Is everything okay?" He appreciates Robin's genuine concern.

"I'm so sorry. I've been overseeing a huge work project that is taking up all my time," Alex says.

"I totally understand that work projects are your priority. I can certainly relate because I've been in your shoes many times too," Robin replies.

She describes to Alex her process for letting the CEO know about board members' planned attendance. Prior to each board meeting, the CEO provides the chair a list of board members who RSVP'd and those who informed the CEO why they wouldn't be able to make the upcoming meeting. This list is important because Robin and the CEO need to know who won't be part of important topics that will be discussed and how to best keep everyone abreast of the board's vital work.

"I understand better now. I didn't realize my attendance mattered so much. I also now get why it's so important to let you know when I won't be able to make it," he says.

"We always want you to know you're a valued member of the board. We realize how hard you work to raise money. And we just want to let you know you're missed and we care. If your project is still ongoing, feel free to give us a heads-up because your absence makes sense, but we hope to see you at the next meeting," Robin says.

Alex appreciates the call and her offer to help. He attends all meetings for the rest of the year without the chair or CEO having to ever bring up, let alone pull, the go trigger.

In another scenario, upon further investigation sometimes we realize the board member's lack of commitment stems from his or her motives. A volunteer may be more interested in building a résumé or professional networking through board membership than meeting the nonprofit's purpose. This is often the case with volunteers who struggle to meet their obligations. We try our hardest to support them, but despite all our attempts to improve their performance, we see little if any effort and change for the better on their part. While adding to one's CV and creating connections are rewarding benefits of volunteer work, when they're a person's primary objectives, then performance and attendance may be less of a priority.

I also always appreciate volunteers who say, "I just need time. If you could stick by me, I would appreciate it. But if you need to let me go, I understand." In those instances, we often did our best to keep those honest, caring people on board. Finding amazing volunteers that fit a specific need for the nonprofit is a tremendous amount of work. So once we found one, we did our utmost to adapt to their life circumstances in order to have them stay engaged.

In another scenario, imagine Tiffany is raising forty thousand dollars instead of her annual give and get amount of ten thousand dollars, but she's been absent from the last three meetings. Her commitment to the nonprofit is clear. Her giving of her treasure is way above her initial pledge. But when it comes to her time, she is missing the mark. So rather than kick her off the board because of her poor attendance record, I'll first go about finding out why her giving of treasure is exceeding that of her time and talent. By expressing our interest in her participation and identifying the cause of her absences, the board chair and I may be able to provide her the support she needs to improve her participation.

My leadership approach is rooted in facts and optimism. When the facts via the scorecards indicate underperformance, I interpret the data through a positive lens. Experience has taught me that volunteers miss meetings for legitimate reasons. If I believe that each volunteer is important and has been appointed to fill a particular need within the board, then it's the duty of the board chair and me to find the cause of missed meetings and to be as understanding, accommodating, and helpful as possible.

Fully Present but Financially Struggling Volunteers: More Time and Talent, Less Treasure

LET'S SAY STEVE HAS A HIGH ATTENDANCE SCORE but he's not meeting his give and get amount. At the same time, he has a perfect attendance record, is on the planning committee for the annual gala, and has been devoting hours and hours to make the evening a success.

Rachel, a current board member, nominated Steve to be on the board. Although Thomas, the board chair, takes on conversations with volunteers who aren't meeting their goals, in this case, he and the CEO determine that Rachel is the best person to take charge. Thomas reaches out to Rachel to receive her opinion. He starts by explaining the problem.

"I'm so glad you told me," Rachel says. "I'm sure having these conversations isn't at the top of your fun list."

"You're right. But I always strive to have them because upholding clear communication is more important than avoiding addressing delicate topics. In the end, I'd rather go to you first with the bad news and receive your input than avoid it and have you find out some other way. You'd be left wondering why we hadn't told you before it was too late to do anything about it," Thomas says.

"Definitely appreciated! Plus this is part ego play for me. Steve's performance reflects on my ability to identify solid prospective volunteers . . . I have my reputation and track record to uphold! I know Steve well, so if it's okay with you, let me get to the bottom of why he's not meeting his goal. From there, we can figure out what we can do," Rachel says.

Without even having to ask for Rachel's help, she offered to be of service. Thomas takes this as a clear sign that the Nominating Committee knows how to bring on hard-working and assertive board members who step up when they see a need.

"Thanks for taking on this responsibility. I know you'll be more effective than I would be, given your friendship with Steve," Thomas says.

Had Rachel said she didn't feel comfortable broaching the subject with Steve, the board chair would have gladly made the call. Thankfully, both Thomas and Rachel agree that she will be the best person to reach out to Steve on the board's behalf.

Using Past Scorecards to Set Future Goals

ON AN ANNUAL BASIS, I use the previous year's scorecard highlights to encourage the present board. At the start of a new board year, I've told my volunteers where our strengths and weaknesses were the prior year. I intentionally speak in broad terms when addressing the board to maintain volunteer confidentiality during this kick-off, celebratory conversation. When your current volunteers see how you're carefully guarding the individual details of your previous board members, they'll understand you'll do the same for them.

In your case, I recommend you craft your message staying positive and using facts, particularly when you're highlighting areas where you seek to strengthen the board. Your board chair is a valuable resource here. Receive his or her input to improve your delivery. In most instances, I've found that the board chair and I agree on the board's strengths and weaknesses and my plan regarding how I will broach this topic with the board.

Keeping high-caliber volunteers engaged over the long term is both a challenge and a prerequisite for strong boards, and strong boards are essential partners you and your staff need to fulfill your nonprofit's mission. While you can be the best CEO in your organization's history, without amazing partners, you'll struggle to create the vital connections within the community that open doors to opportunities your nonprofit needs to compete and grow. The scorecard is not intended to play the intrusive role of drill sergeant or Big Brother. Rather, it quantifies an otherwise vague and subjective volunteer evaluation process. It increases objectivity and provides you a measurable strategy to meet your greatest ambitions. A remarkable board unleashes your potential to elevate your nonprofit to new heights.

Interviews with Your Executive Assistant, Staff, and Donors: Essential Preparation Prior to Your One-on-One Meetings

IMPLEMENTING THE BOARD SCORECARDS will form the foundation of building a highly effective board. They provide you the metrics you need to identify strengths and weaknesses. Next, you'll dig even deeper into assessing your board when you review minutes of the previous year's Nominating Committee meetings when the nonprofit was headed by the prior CEO, as well as meet with your executive assistant and management team regarding the current board and its history. Part of your exhaustive ninety-day fact-finding mission is to learn how the board and the nominating process were organized. Furthermore, key to having informed discussions with your chair, individual volunteers and donors, and corporate and foundation sponsors is to do your homework prior to your one-on-one meetings. This gains you credibility.

Within most nonprofits, the EAs, management team, and departments have essential details about the current board, individual volunteers and donors, and corporate and foundation sponsors. EAs typically recorded Nominating Committee minutes with the CEO (in your case the previous CEO), and the management team and departments have key details as well.

The following are questions to answer prior to your one-on-one meetings with your chair, individual volunteers and donors, and corporate and foundation sponsors:

Questions to ask yourself

To begin, consider the following items and discuss them with your EA, who likely has insight you lack for these issues, before your one-on-one meetings. In my experience, EAs have been my secret weapon for insider information. While never my sole source, their insights are valuable and the fast-track to learning about the inner workings of the nonprofit. From your informal talk with your EA, think deeply through each with ambition, conviction, and an open mind; in this way, you are unlocking massive potential. The names of those who emerge from your answers will dramatically expand your network of those who will contribute greatly to your nonprofit:

- Are there any local or national peer groups that you should tap into? *At the local level, examples include non-profit associations for executives, state alliances for non-profit organizations, and other federations that advocate for funding from state governments and track proposed legislation that, if enacted into law, will affect nonprofits.*
- Are there any associations or memberships you belong to that you wish to remain on while coming into this role? *Such groups are important because they may provide work and personal balance in your life. In my case, it was my participation in Young Presidents' Organization (YPO).*
- Who are the must-see donors that you need to meet with? *These individuals not only support your cause financially, but they also bring support from their peer group. They are committed investors in your nonprofit's mission.*

- Are there any major volunteers or donors or both that no longer support the organization due to a fallout or misunderstanding? If so, as a new CEO not connected to prior conflicts, consider how you can mend these broken bonds.

General questions about your board of directors

- What is the Nominating Committee timeline to recruit and search for new board members annually? (The importance of this question depends on when you were hired.)
- Is there a process in the organization as to how a person ascends to various volunteer leadership roles?
- How has board recruitment taken place, and who has been responsible for this task?
- What do the bylaws state about Nominating Committee activities, and what materials are used to make these decisions annually?
- What is the board's demographic makeup?
- Is the job description for being a board member documented and referred to in the bylaws? What do the bylaws say are a board member's roles, responsibilities, and committee assignments?
- What type of board orientation takes place for board members, and during which month does the board orientation occur?
- When exactly was the organization's bylaws last updated? Who led this effort from the board when the update was done?

- When did the last board retreat take place?
- Is there an updated strategic plan, and are there current board members who were a part of the process of developing it?
- Are there board members that can provide you with historical perspectives about the organization?
- Which board members can objectively provide you the nonprofit's pros and cons?

Questions about the chair

Prior to addressing these questions, ask yourself, "What expectations do I have, and what planning will I do with the current and future chairs?" When answering this question, think about how you'll partner and work with the current and future board chairs to run your nonprofit and execute your ambitious vision.

- What responsibilities and connections to groups outside of the nonprofit does your chair have?
- How long has the chair been on the board of directors?
- How long does the chair serve in this role?
- Before becoming the chair, how long had this person been engaged with the organization?
- Is there any story or background about the board chair's appointment that will help me connect with him or her and guide our one-on-one-meeting?
- Does he or she have the proper prerequisites and training to serve as chair? Prerequisites and training include the chair's:

- knowledge of running meetings;
- public-speaking mastery;
- understanding of *Robert's Rules of Order*, including protocols for approving board minutes and policies;
- experience working with the CEO in preparing items to be covered at each board meeting and in developing and providing an annotated agenda to conduct each meeting;
- preference to have additional notes for the meeting or not;
- steps that he or she will take ahead of time to inform the CEO to lead various portions of the board meeting when such a need arises.

Questions about individual volunteers

- What responsibilities and connections to any group outside of the nonprofit does your volunteer have?
- What year did the board member begin?
- What is the board member's business background such as law, banking, business, construction, media, etc.?
- What is the board member's individual giving for each of the last five years?

Questions about individual donors

Your nonprofit most likely has an annual giving society or similar recognition program in place. You probably researched this during the hiring process prior to your CEO appointment. If this is the case, then you already have a solid handle on the donors you will arrange one-on-one meetings with during your first ninety days. My recommendation is that you meet with your top ten in terms of financial contribution.

As you prepare for your one-on-one meetings, learn as much as you can about the giving society or recognition program, which is often described in annual reports or the nonprofit's website or both. Through your research and the questions you'll ask of your staff and management team, you'll find information about your major donors far beyond merely the names of individuals, corporations, and foundations. You'll learn their giving history and clues to their personality, such as what guides their contribution of time, talent, or treasure or a combination of these three. Use this information to develop your approach to maintaining their loyalty and appeal for increased giving. Furthermore, by learning about your nonprofit's giving society or recognition program, you'll gain insight into the strengths and weaknesses of its strategy to add new donors.

- What responsibilities and connections to any group outside of the nonprofit does your donor have?
- What staff member or department or both has the information associated with the annual giving society or similar recognition program? *Once you have this information, study it.*
- Who are the top-ten contributors of your individual annual giving society?
- What will be your plan to visit your top-ten donors in the first ninety days?

- Are any top-ten donors on your board of directors? *If so, prepare for your one-on-one meetings by using the three Ts and the donor's history of support as a board member to guide your one-on-one meeting.*
- What aspects of your vision for the nonprofit's future are relevant to your individual donors? *Plan to describe these to them.*
- Does your nonprofit have a major gifts staff member who can provide you specific details about each of these individuals and couples? If not, who has this information and which staff member has the best relationship with each individual and couple?
- Ask your staff and board chair, "Whom should I meet with in the first ninety days?" *Compare these names to the ones you came up with prior to seeking their input.*
- Are there different affinity groups tied to annual fundraising events the nonprofit organizes? What are the levels of giving at these events? Do these contributions count toward the annual giving society recognition for individual donor recognition?
- Does your national organization (through its donor-recognition program) recognize major donors in your local community for their generosity? If yes, does the national organization hold any events to bring these generous donors together? How does this recognition program work?
- Has the nonprofit given your donors any awards that have recognized them and demonstrated your nonprofit's appreciation? If so, what are the details—who received the awards, when, and for what?

Questions about corporate and foundation donors

You'll evaluate your corporate and foundation sponsors similar to your individual donors. Thus I recommend you meet with your top-ten corporate and foundation supporters in order of their financial contribution.

- What events, programs, capital projects, or unrestricted gifts of support do your corporate and foundation supporters provide to serve your clients?
- What amount of giving does your nonprofit require to be an event sponsor at the highest levels?
- How does the organization recognize a corporation's or foundation's contributions to the organization?
- Does the organization have sponsorship packages to solicit support?
- Who are the key contacts for each corporation and foundation? *For corporations, the person is often a community relations representative, and for foundations, the person is often the CEO.*
- Within each corporation and foundation providing funding, who is the person or people you want to meet with regarding the entity's financial support?
- For each foundation, what are the names of the trustees who make funding decisions? Do any of your board members know them, and were they the ones who helped secure this support? **People give to people.** *Thus tell the background story of how commitments of time, talent, and treasure were made. To be able to describe such information in an engaging and sincere way shows that you, as the new CEO, respect and value the relationships*

that have been built and that you'll eagerly champion and continue the nonprofit's proud legacy.
- For each corporation and foundation, how do you meet with and thank the highest-ranking executive for his or her support? How do you thank the trustees of these entities who approved the gifts to be provided?
- What requirements does the company or foundation have for nonprofits to request donations?
- Does your nonprofit have a grant writer who maintains relationships with corporate and foundation supporters?
- Does any resource development or special event staff have the relationship with corporate or foundation staff to secure annual support for events or programs?
- Is the nonprofit required to make its donation request or appeal within a specific timeframe? If so, when are the deadlines?
- Does one or more of your corporate or foundation supporters have representation on your board of directors? If yes, what kind of insight can these board members provide you regarding the support from their organization?

Masterfully Conducting Your One-on-One Meetings

FOR EACH OF THE ONE-ON-ONE MEETINGS you will have as the new CEO, keep this simple goal in mind: *Get to know and become closer to the person you meet!*

Remember that **people give to people**. The stronger the bond you create with your volunteers and donors, the more trust you build and credibility you earn. A big part of meeting the straightforward but time-consuming task of getting to know and becoming closer to each group is to do your homework. In this section, we'll refer to your volunteers and individual, foundation, and corporate donors as **contributors**.

Your Resource Development Department often has a file for each contributor. In this instance, research this file and ask your EA and staff for any other information that will provide you background of the contributor's history of giving and involvement with the nonprofit. Also, search online to uncover any current articles or social media content about your contributors. See if other organizations have recognized any of them or if their family members have received awards for their philanthropy and volunteer work. You'll use what you discover as a guide and to connect with your contributors during your one-on-one meetings.

Five Steps to an Effective Meeting

YOUR TIME AND YOUR CONTRIBUTORS' TIME are valuable. So to ensure you conduct the most successful meeting possible, time management is key. Follow these five steps to ensure your meetings are efficient and accomplish your objective of getting to know and become closer to each person:

1. Create a Warm Introduction

There's no need to do a cold call with the contributor as the new CEO. When you have the right people to introduce you before you make your first contact with the donor, take advantage of this opportunity. These could be members from the Search Committee, board members, friends who initially introduced this person to your organization, or staff who can make the introduction happen because of the relationship they have built over time with the donor.

2. Don't Go Solo; Invite a Friend or Associate to Join You

The person who arranged your warm introduction may also be the best person to accompany you on your first call. If this individual isn't able, I still suggest taking someone with you to the one-on-one meeting. Options include a Search Committee member, a board member, a person from the donor's company who is involved with your nonprofit, or a staff person who may know the donor because of the gift he or she made for a program the contributor supports. Having a third person in your first meeting just makes everyone feel more comfortable and keeps a conversation flowing.

3. First Impressions Are a Great Start to New Relationships

The initial impact you make during your one-on-one meetings will be crucial for the start of a productive relationship. A comprehensive strategy is key to building successful connections you want to have as the new CEO.

I remember a first meeting with a contributor. Prior to our one-on-one, I discovered a key fact about Max when conducting my research. He had been in the military and used the GI bill to pay for college. When I brought up his military service during our meeting and asked him about this aspect of his life, we created an immediate bond. I enjoyed learning about his deployments, and he had fascinating stories to tell. Members of my own family had proudly served our country, and I expressed my admiration and gratitude for his commitment to our nation. He in turn appreciated my interest.

Max shared that without the GI Bill, he wouldn't have been able to attend college because the financial hardship would have been too great. Graduating with his bachelor's opened opportunities that allowed him to lead his best life that eventually created his wealth and philanthropic interests. I tapped into his passion to give back by discussing my role as the new CEO and my ambitious vision for the nonprofit. By aligning Max's time, talent, and treasure with what our organization needed, I presented him with a personalized win-win proposition. Researching about Max prior to our meeting helped forge a bond that deepened over time and benefitted our nonprofit immensely.

4. Always Say Thank You

I send a handwritten thank-you note after every meeting within twenty-four hours. Some people prefer sending an email, but I believe receiving a handwritten note has become a memorable event these days. Anyone can rattle away an email in minutes, but a handwritten note says you took the time to express your appreciation and stands apart from the emails that flood inboxes every day.

5. Think in the Long Term

Always conclude your contributor meetings with your next step in mind. Your subsequent step could be a tour of one of your programs the contributor supports or sending the person information about the work being done. You could invite him or her to be your guest at an upcoming event your organization is hosting to raise funds. Or you could invite the individual to be a guest speaker at a board or staff meeting regarding his or her involvement. Always be creative in how you make the contributor feel special and connected to your work. Your top contributors are often smart, highly successful, and generous people, so see how you can tap into their enthusiasm and desire to share their talents. As the new CEO, be engaging, enthusiastic, and grateful for their involvement.

Key Questions to Ask Your Contributors

Throughout each meeting, remind yourself that people *love* talking about themselves! And the more you spark conversation, the more you'll engender trust and gain credibility. The following are potential questions to ask during your initial meeting with each generous contributor to get things going on the call. They both deepen your understanding of each person, which is key to your fundraising efforts, and facilitate your one-on-one conversations. Also, you know your nonprofit best, so be sure to modify these questions and add more that will align with the needs you've identified within your organization:

- Why did you initially decide to make a gift to us?
- Is there a personal connection you have to our mission? Can you share a little about that with me?
- What about the nonprofit's mission is important to you?
- What do you like most and least about our nonprofit?
- How do we work with you and treat you, compared to other organizations you support? What can we do better for you now and into the future?

- How do you think we are perceived in the community?
- What would motivate you to continue your support and give more time, talent, or treasure or all three in the future?
- *For non-volunteer contributors:* Are you engaged with us beyond your generous gift to the organization?
- *For non-volunteer contributors:* Do you see yourself becoming more engaged with the organization beyond your current activity?

The answers to the questions throughout this chapter will guide your plan to bring about lasting change within your nonprofit. Your meetings will point out strengths within your organization, which you'll use to deliver upon the promises you made that led to your hire. They will also identify problems you'll need to fix, which would otherwise impede your progress. Your nonprofit's strengths and weaknesses will guide your strategy moving forward.

Now that you've learned about Framework 1, let's see real-world examples of how they'll solve your biggest problems and pour the foundation for your long-term success.

Chapter 8

Framework 1: Ninety Days— Three Case Studies

> In this chapter, you'll read how, as a new CEO of three nonprofits, I successfully applied the ninety-day strategy. Each of the following case studies illustrates a specific lesson:
>
> - The importance of meeting the agencies you fund
> - The power of one-on-one meetings
> - Repairing a fractured relationship

SEEING IS BELIEVING. While I've explained how Framework 1 works, providing examples of my experiences as a nonprofit CEO and how I applied the practices you've learned about will allow you to see their real-world application. In the following three case studies, you'll see how I implemented the first ninety-day practices into the organizations I led.

Case Study 1
The Benefits of Meeting with Agencies We Funded

AT THIRTY-FIVE YEARS OLD, I was among the youngest CEOs in this nonprofit's system when I was hired by the local board of directors to lead what was one of the top fifty entities in the national organization, each one raising millions of dollars annually in its community. This local nonprofit covers three counties in the state. Combined, the tri-county area had a twenty-seven-million-dollar budget at the time with a staff of over forty people that supported seventy-five agencies and 180 programs with a board of directors of over seventy members. It was my first experience leading a nonprofit and a major career leap from my prior position. I was thrilled to push myself to new professional heights.

For the previous nine years, I had been in the organization's system in two other states. With one, I was the assistant campaign director, and with the other, I was the vice president of Resource Development and Workplace Services. Although I had worked with the organization in other states, I was an outsider CEO as far as this local nonprofit was concerned. And unlike my previous position, my wife and I had never lived in this state and had no personal or professional ties to it. I was even overlooked in the first round of interviews. After completing the initial interviews of other applicants, the Search Committee called me stating they had probably moved too quickly in their recruitment process when they had skipped over me. Now in their second stage, they asked if I would be interested in coming in for a visit and interview. With zero hesitation I said yes, and the rest is history.

I needed to quickly learn as much as possible about my new community and earn credibility within it. Thus from day one, I began arranging my group and one-on-one meetings to fully understand my organization and the area it served.

At this nonprofit, I determined the primary groups and individuals I needed to meet with during my first ninety days. I scheduled meetings with my direct reports and their staff, along with seventy-five agency executives, and those that led the programs we funded within their agencies. So meetings with my staff and the agency group were my focus in my first ninety days. I identified top donors who supported the annual campaign and set times to meet with them, along with my board members. But given all the individuals and groups I needed to meet with, my meetings didn't stop at the three-month mark. Beyond the ninety days, I met with top donors and board members.

In chapter 4, "Framework 1: Whom Do I Meet during My First Ninety Days?" and chapter 5. "Framework 1: One-on-One Meetings during Your First Ninety Days," we took a deep dive into meeting with each of these groups. For this case study, I'll focus on the seventy-five agencies that the nonprofit funded and their executives. Keep in mind that my approach to meeting these agencies is similar to how I met with other groups.

In my positions prior to this one as CEO, I had worked in resource development and fundraising where I had developed a solid track record for bringing in money. Given the importance placed on CEOs to procure money in this national organization, my background gave me much-needed fundraising expertise. As a first-time CEO, I had fought hard to land the position, and I had a fire in my belly. The nonprofit was providing support to the seventy-five agencies with 180 programs being funded through the Annual Campaign in unrestricted funding through the Community Allocation Committee Process.

In my first ninety days, I made a personal and public promise to visit every single agency executive who was a partner and stakeholder. My intent was to understand and gain firsthand knowledge of the programs being funded. I made my announcement at my first monthly meeting with agency executives and the leadership team. Within the local nonprofit, the CEO, agency executives, and leadership team met every month to discuss the work being done by the agency community. My ambitious pledge instantly caught every agency executive's attention during my inaugural meeting. Unfortunately, some agency executives that received our funding didn't attend the monthly meetings. I wanted to solve this problem. One person asked if I was planning to meet with these absentee agency executives as well.

"That's the goal! If you got funding from us, you'll be getting a visit," I replied.

So how was Brian, the new guy, going to get absentee executives engaged with the group and from now on to attend the monthly meetings? Part of my solution was to ask the staff who worked directly with the agencies why they believed these people were not attending the monthly meetings. I used this information to help guide my conversations with these particular professionals. With my direct approach, I signaled that a new day for the organization had begun.

Without even visiting, I had my first point to consider—how to strengthen potential agency relationships among the group. This shows how information can come to you quickly by enacting Framework 1.

My staff initially thought I had set an audacious goal. They were right! But my wonderful executive assistant was fully on board. She loved the challenge and declared we would reach the ninety-day goal. She started the process to get me on the calendar of each agency—big and small—throughout the tri-county area.

My direct reports were also supportive of my plan. On the other hand, some of the leaders who worked closely with the agencies had their doubts. Without telling me, some probably thought I would not meet my ninety-day goal. By informing the nonprofit's key board members of my intentions during the interview process, my promise had created a lot of buzz and conversation about the new CEO. I was referred to as the former development guy that was actually making his first priority to visit every agency the organization funded. Many people in the nonprofit world don't make the connection between great fundraising and knowing exactly what you're selling. I had unlocked this secret years ago. Thus being a powerful fundraiser was going to make me an even better CEO for my organization.

In and of itself, driving to my meetings with agency executives in the tri-county area was informative. I learned where the agency was located and the socioeconomic status of the neighborhoods my nonprofit supported. Kicking the tires, so to speak, and knowing about communities are key to addressing their greatest needs when raising money to improve them. During the appointments themselves, I learned about people on their home turf, which provided them a level of comfort that encouraged open, candid conversation. They provided vital insight that they would most likely not have expressed had we not met face-to-face.

During our conversation, they shared what they appreciated about having a program that our nonprofit funded. They also described the weaknesses of our current partnership and the nonprofit as a whole, including prior decisions they disagreed with and the board leadership. The executives regularly described whom they enjoyed working with and whom they didn't. If a staff person's name came up as a great person to work with, I noted this and shared the good news with the individual. I took this as an opportunity to recognize the person immediately for his or her work and commitment, as well as potential for professional growth further benefitting my organization.

If a name consistently came up negatively, I would investigate more to confirm the validity of the criticisms. If I corroborated the claims, I would address the problem.

I also learned about common donors who gave to the agencies that received our funding and those who also supported us. Donors who supported us and the agency believed in both the nonprofit's and the funding agency's missions to meet local needs, which were evaluated through the agency allocation review process. While our funding was restricted to a certain program or programs within an agency, these donors could also provide the following:

- Unrestricted dollars to the agency
- Money to the programs the nonprofit was funding
- Contributions to programs the nonprofit was not funding but was operating within the agency
- Sponsorship of a fundraising event for the agency to raise additional dollars for its mission-critical work

This was all valuable information I was learning firsthand as the new CEO.

During my meetings, I discovered that no prior CEOs had visited all the agency executives' operations as I was doing. Upon further research, I found out only the agencies that received the highest funding and profile earned a visit. I also received helpful tips on whom else I should meet that I had not considered before.

Many agencies highlighted my visits in their own donor communications and welcomed me with banners and kids participating in their programs putting on short, entertaining performances as part of the tour. They clearly appreciated that I was taking time out of my schedule to see their work.

After one tour, I received the no-nonsense appeal: What were my plans to grow the annual campaign? Specifically, agencies were dealing with program issues and needed a comprehensive information-and-referral service to connect people needing agency help in the tri-county area. In addition, the nonprofit needed a permanent home. All were fair points, and if I were in their position, I would have probably had the same concerns.

Twenty years after my first meeting with one agency executive, I ran into him at a national conference. Tim described how he regularly talked to his staff, volunteers, and other leaders regarding the high level of interest I had taken in his agency's work and how I personally got to know the other agencies like his that I met with. He appreciated the time I took to have a one-on-one meeting with him within my first ninety days to learn more about his program that we funded at the time.

"I tell everyone how my experience with you was one of the best I've had with a funding executive," he told me.

What a great feeling to know the outcome still lived on in his mind decades after our first meeting!

I also was thankful for Tim at that initial meeting. He let me know who were the organization's allies and detractors, as well as brought needs and concerns to my attention. I used this information to develop a plan to address them. He and other agency executives consistently gave me an open invitation to visit them.

When there was a change in executive leadership at one of our funded agencies, I did my best to pay a timely visit to welcome the new person to the community. This was a great way to let someone new know that we were glad to have him or her as a part of the community. I always let the new executive know to call me if he or she needed my support.

Case Study 2
One Meeting Results in a World-Class Program Serving the US Military

DURING MY FIRST NINETY DAYS, I began one-on-one meetings with staff in the various departments of the local chapter of this national humanitarian organization. The operation itself was large and included several satellite locations throughout the counties we covered in two states.

My meetings were not only with my direct reports but also with individuals who were directors within their various departments. In addition, I had group meetings with staff by departments over lunch, as you learned about in chapter 4, "Framework 1: Whom Do I Meet during My First Ninety Days?"

During one of those meetings, Kristen, a department employee, told me, "Mr. Quail, this is my first time ever being invited to the CEO's conference room, and I've been with the organization for about five years."

Kristen expressed how meaningful my invitation had been to her. Prior to hearing this, I had no idea what a big deal this would be for her. Others also described a similar degree of gratitude for these appointments either directly to me or to staff members who told me later.

Our meeting was a memorable moment for both Kristen and me because it was a sign of positive change I was bringing to the nonprofit. My meeting with Kristen and her department reminded me that simple positive acts can make a huge difference in how people will perform in their jobs. Employees appreciate when their contributions to the nonprofit are acknowledged by those at the top of the organization.

But not all the feedback I received was positive. Some of my direct reports questioned why I was meeting with the rank and file that were several layers down from the top. I thought it both interesting and sad how my efforts to get to know the staff and gain their trust could be interpreted as negative or even threatening to their authority. Meanwhile, other direct reports appreciated my effort that sent a great message to employees that I was an accessible leader who valued their work.

Such a mixed bag of reactions reflects human nature. The negative interpretation of my ninety-day plan demonstrates our tendency to be skeptical of others if not downright mistrustful: "What's his ulterior motive behind wanting to meet with *my* direct reports?" "Will anything he finds out reflect poorly on me?" "Doesn't he have better things to do than to meddle in my business?"

At the same time, I understood their concern because the board leadership hired me to be the new boss to make improvements, which required me to dig into the work of my direct reports. They might have felt threatened by such investigations that came from my need to learn so much about the various programs and the people who ran my direct reports' departments.

Regardless, I have found meetings with those in the lower ranks beneficial. The employees working for my direct reports have usually been honest and candid about the needs they have identified within the nonprofit. These rank-and-file meetings also helped me evaluate if I wanted to keep certain people on the senior management team whom the last CEO of over eighteen years had appointed.

But sometimes responses suggested not all was being revealed. Seemingly overly optimistic statements would catch my attention and motivate me to find out more. For example I heard, "Everything is running great and I am all good." This might have been true . . . or the person might have been reassuring me so I wouldn't dig deeper.

Another type of statement that caught my attention was when a person disclosed a detail that implied more than the stated words. In other words, this was possibly a passive attempt to tell me something beyond what I had asked about. One director said to me during our one-on-one meeting, "I have less than a year left until I retire."

I immediately questioned how hard she would work for the remainder of her time in her position. Upon further inquiry, I later learned she had been a loyal employee for decades, was proud of her service, and always took her work seriously. So you always need to balance your snap judgments with a need to get to know people more fully.

Because these people you are meeting with have their new leader in front of them, they may take this time to describe their successes, areas they are currently operating, and the importance of a particular project they're working on. They may be saying this not just for their own self-aggrandizement but also to lobby for themselves and the people they serve and to express a problem they think you can help solve or services, programs, or changes they think you'll support with your expertise and resources. This is exactly what happened with Karen, a director who told me about her ambitious vision to provide a much-needed service and the resources she needed to execute her plan within our nonprofit.

Karen ran our local program that connected military members with their families during times of personal crisis. Our national organization, through its federal charter with the government, has a special legal status called "federal instrumentality" that allows it to carry out responsibilities the government has delegated to it. One of these duties is to provide family communications and other forms of support to the US military.

The national organization provides the emergency messaging for the military with news from home to a soldier in the field regarding a death in the family, the birth of a child, or a request for a loved one to be with family members during such events. The military uses the national organization and its chapters to verify such events in order to authorize or deny military personnel to return home.

The hard-working director was running a twenty-four-hour, year-round operation for the local nonprofit when I came on board. Karen also did the work for smaller chapters within the state and various other states under individual chapter contractual agreements where our staff handled these military service calls for a fee, which enabled our chapter to provide the service as a part of its operations.

These chapters—both small and large—contracted with the local nonprofit. They were responsible to be there for service members and their families. By working with us, they were meeting their chapter obligation to serve their community. Once a month, we billed those chapters for the work we performed per our agreement. The director and her team were generating revenue for the organization and providing mission-critical work.

During our one-on-one meeting, Karen lamented how she felt unappreciated because she and her team were generating revenue but could not get new software, equipment, dedicated space within the building, and other items she needed to make her department run like a true, efficient call center handling a large volume of calls.

"If we were able to provide those resources, could we build this to scale and take on more chapters?" I asked her.

"Definitely!" she said.

When I visited the room handling these calls, I agreed with her complaint. She and her team—all dedicated employees who believed in the mission—were on top of each other in a cramped space that was clearly too small for them. During daily shift changes, the person beginning work sat down in the same chair of the one being relieved. Because the two shifts shared the same desk, I saw photos of two different families at the same workstation. Based on the team's need to expand this critical service to achieve an effective outcome, it required more support and resources. Furthermore, one thing Karen told me hit a homerun:

"I had once been on the other side of receiving the message when a family member was in the military. I know what it means for this message to be sent and be verified because my family was affected and my family member was able to make it home before a loved one passed away."

This is an example of a memorable moment that I would later share with my board members to remind them of the importance of their volunteer work.

In Karen's case, she did this work because of what the service had done for her, and she was determined to give back and have, in her words, "the best center delivering these messages in the country."

By contracting with us, other chapters would be able to fully leverage their resources. They would be able to focus on other important needs of their local nonprofit chapter within their communities. I saw this as a win-win proposition. That day, Karen let me know about a need for a true call center and her enthusiasm to help create one. Her passion provided the spark of inspiration that eventually led to establishing a legitimate call center.

Karen's words were all I needed to hear because they connected with my previous experience setting up a call center for information and referral services while I was CEO at the three-county nonprofit mentioned in the first case. I knew the value and the possibilities of having one, but more importantly, I had this petite woman with giant passion, desire, and drive to take her department to the next level. And her positive energy motivated me to provide her the resources she needed to accomplish her ambitious goals.

From this one-on-one meeting, we developed a twenty-four-person call center operating year-round and twenty-four hours a day at the local nonprofit. What had been a storage area for used furniture within the lower level of our building, we converted into a huge call center.

We were able to get board members excited about seeing how this mission-critical service could extend to other communities via additional chapters of the national organization throughout the United States. My board and management team were eager to help us establish this call center.

From eighty-four chapters at the time, we expanded our contracts to two hundred covering seventy million people throughout the country. When I departed this nonprofit, we were handling over three thousand military cases per month via service calls. Its annual budget of $775,000 generated $100,000 of income delivering these vital messages. We used that revenue to purchase the equipment and resources to remain on top of our game.

My one-on-one appointment sparked epic changes in our delivery service system. It was indeed a memorable moment, not just for me but also for the thousands of lives touched by the vital work our call center performed.

The national organization now supports and operates three call centers, of which this is one. Combined, they cover all the military messaging for the entire country. This has lifted the burden from local chapters to provide this service within their organizations.

Solving an enormous problem within our chapter helped other chapters. We showed the national organization that ours could handle calls faster and more efficiently than each chapter doing it on its own. At the same time, chapters that used our call center met their obligations to the national organization.

The original center lives on today and provides an invaluable service that makes a positive difference in people's lives. It's one of the proudest legacies of my CEO career. My hope is that your one-on-one meetings will result in similar success for your nonprofit.

Case Study 3
Repairing a Broken Relationship

EARLY ON AS CEO, I LEARNED from several board members about one important donor of a foundation with a long and loyal history with the local nonprofit. For reasons no one could clearly explain to me, the foundation was donating to only one of our programs, whereas for most of its history with us, it had supported the entire nonprofit. I wanted to get to the bottom of its decision in hopes to persuade this extremely generous foundation to revert to its original funding plan.

I set up a meeting with the foundation's CEO, Jerome. Prior to this appointment with the CEO, I performed intel within my nonprofit. But whenever I asked what happened, I received vague answers from my direct reports and board members. Some blamed the previous executive leadership for messing up the relationship, while others said they weren't sure what had caused the fracture between the two organizations. Based on my CEO experience, I had a feeling people knew more than they were telling me because no one provided me a straightforward answer, and this raised a red flag for me. My suspicions would later prove to be correct.

I then phoned the foundation's CEO directly. Typically, I have my EA schedule these appointments. But in this case, I made the phone call because the strained relationship between our nonprofit and the foundation meant no one in my nonprofit could perform a warm introduction on my behalf. These introductory calls were usually easy and friendly because of the solid relationship between the nonprofit and CEOs that supported us. Throughout our short talk, however, Jerome maintained a somewhat frosty, all-business but cordial tone that signaled to me some tension between our two organizations.

"Yes, we can meet. I'll have one of my board members there to provide you background history of our support of your nonprofit," he said.

Jerome also provided me the board member's name. I appreciated this information because I would use it to research and better prepare for our first meeting.

After our call, I asked my staff if they knew who this board member was. I found out she was a very well-connected person in the community who knew many of our board members. She had helped the nonprofit get in touch with the family that wound up making one of the biggest donations in our history at the time. The more I dug, the more complicated the problem between our organizations seemed. Meanwhile, no one had provided me a clear answer explaining the problem and what had gone wrong.

The day of our meeting, I arrived at the foundation's office. As Jerome had told me, his board member, Jennifer, was there. Jennifer started off by giving me a brief overview of the history of our partnership and the support that was provided to our organization. According to her account, we had made promises, as outlined in an agreement between us and the family, that evidently we had not fulfilled. Jerome remained quiet and left the talking to Jennifer and me.

"Have you reviewed this agreement?" Jennifer asked.

Given that our history with the foundation spanned over a decade and it was one of our biggest donors, the question made sense. To my chagrin, no one on my staff had mentioned this document to me, despite the fact-finding mission I'd performed prior to this meeting. As a CEO who prided himself on always preparing for appointments, particularly important ones like this, I was embarrassed and upset that I looked ill prepared and even incompetent through no fault of my own. At all costs, I always avoided being caught off-guard. However, I still owned the fact that I had not been prepared. I apologized for not having read the document.

Jennifer's response was that staff could surely provide me with the document and that plenty of people still on the board could probably highlight what terms in the agreement we had not met. While I didn't show it, hearing that my staff had possibly withheld key information from me disappointed and frustrated me. I certainly would be asking my team about this document as soon as possible.

"I'm sincerely sorry for what took place. Thank you for bringing this to my attention, and I'll ask my staff to locate the agreement, and I will review it immediately. Would you consider meeting again after I get to the bottom of what happened?" I asked.

"Of course," Jennifer said. "But from here on out, I'll have you and Jerome meet. He'll keep me abreast of anything I need to know," she said.

Our meeting lasted an hour and a half. I thanked them for their time.

"My hope is to regain the confidence and trust of your foundation so we can once again receive your support for the broader mission of the entire organization," I said.

Once I had provided my reassurance, Jerome abruptly broke his silence that he had held up to this point.

"That will never happen under my watch!" he said.

The uncomfortable stillness after was as awkward as when I had confessed that I had not read the document. Jerome's sharp statement rattled my nerves a bit at the time. But I would later learn that his harsh words were well deserved, based on the nonprofit's lack of professionalism prior to my CEO appointment.

"I'm thankful for your time, and I appreciate your honesty. Knowing the full gravity of the problem, I can now go about solving it," I said.

My conciliatory words softened Jerome's stance, and he apologized for his bluntness. I reassured him that no apology was necessary. In fact, it was our organization that needed to say sorry if we had not met our obligations outlined in the agreement. Both thanked me for the productive meeting.

"We obviously took you for granted, and now it's my job to show you that I will not be that type of leader," I said.

As a new CEO, my staff had already let me down. They had put my credibility into question by not fully preparing me to meet with one of our most important donors.

Following that meeting, I had a day of reckoning with my direct reports. I asked why they hadn't told me about the document. I received another round of excuses, none of which was credible, especially given the first round of smoke screens they had generated prior to my meeting with Jerome and Jennifer. The agreement appeared on my desk a couple of days later. I reviewed it and saw the terms Jennifer had described we had not met.

In subsequent weeks and months, I went about aggressively healing the trust the nonprofit had broken with the foundation. My investigation based on Jerome's critique caused me to uncover greater problems within the nonprofit that I needed to fix. Stirring up this hornet's nest was difficult but absolutely necessary, and I was thankful for Jerome's honesty. I had to make sure the nonprofit would never repeat the same mistakes again. Part of my efforts required me to make some staffing changes that I believed were holding our nonprofit back.

Restoring the foundation's trust and its financial support took several years. From the start, I established clear, transparent, and consistent communication. I regularly kept Jerome abreast of the new projects I had received funding for that I was overseeing. After showing Jerome how these programs improved the lives of our clients, I then let him know that all our locations were benefiting from these programs but there was an opportunity to do more.

I also sought his feedback regarding the nonprofit's work. While I appreciated his recommendations, critiques, advice, and support, and I never explicitly appealed for more donations. Rather, my goal was to show the foundation our standard of excellence under my leadership and make the case for why I needed additional support to provide more opportunities for our clients through these programs. Jerome had a board he reported to, and they were the ones who ultimately decided on final funding decisions. At the same time, they looked to him for recommendations. Thus Jerome's endorsement or lack thereof made the difference between our program that would receive funding and one that wouldn't.

Over time, I successfully earned the foundation and Jerome's trust. Eventually, we received millions of dollars in donations from it over the course of my tenure focused on these programs that I highlighted above, along with other requests. Jerome and I forged a strong nonprofit-donor partnership. We worked closely together to meet the needs of our community, and he became one of my closest donor allies. In fact, we occasionally joked about that icy first meeting.

As Abraham Lincoln said, "I don't like that man. I must get to know him better." I initially bristled when Jerome abruptly rejected my efforts to regain the foundation's confidence. But I took that on as a challenge. Burning bridges has never been my leadership strategy. I knew doing my utmost to fix mistakes done prior to my tenure would benefit the nonprofit over the long run.

When starting on any CEO job, I always dive into the biggest challenges first. Sometimes you don't even know what they are until one of your most important donors points them out to you! This highlights the importance of the one-on-one meetings that provide you priceless information. Taking on the huge, demanding obstacles right away shows those inside and outside your organization your strength, commitment, and fearlessness to tackle tough topics no one wants to touch.

From fixing broken and fractured donor relationships to dealing with global financial meltdowns, natural disasters, community violence, and worldwide pandemics, leading during difficult times is the test of a CEO's resolve. And the longer you lead, the more challenges you'll face. Framework 1 is your roadmap to building the strongest support network possible inside and outside your nonprofit. With a firm foundation established, you'll set yourself up to succeed throughout your leadership journey.

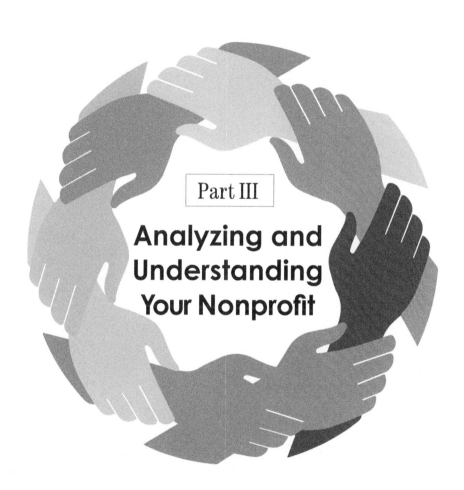

Part III
Analyzing and Understanding Your Nonprofit

Chapter 9

Framework 2: Your Team

> **In this chapter, you'll learn:**
>
> - how to measure the leadership of your direct reports and determine how their role will best fit in your plan for the nonprofit;
> - the importance of your executive assistants—your inside talent assessors, cheerleaders, and advocates;
> - effective strategies to establish trust with board members and benefit from their assessments of your team;
> - the cues team members give to indicate they need to be dismissed;
> - why and how to maintain clear communication lines with the board chair and vice chair;
> - specific questions to ask in assessing your senior managers and their departments.

THERE'S A SAYING IN LEADERSHIP, "Bad news doesn't get better over time and neither do underperforming people." As a leader, facing difficult circumstances and providing powerful solutions is part of what you signed up for when you decided to take on this enormous responsibility. Addressing underperforming or difficult people within your nonprofit is one of the challenges you're charged to deal with during your first year as CEO. Doing so well will require immense skill. In this chapter we'll tackle internal talent assessment head-on, which means you start with your management team.

Have you ever sat in a small, high-level meeting and each time the same person gave you a sinking feeling in your stomach whenever you saw him and heard him speak? Beyond the conference room, you're charged to work closely with him, and you dread each interaction. Now imagine you're a CEO and this person is your direct report who was brought on before you were hired. You'll be stuck working with him while being confident that he's not going to change. Professional experience has taught you this person will be a headache and, more importantly, a major obstacle to accomplishing your big goals. Meanwhile, you're the only one—not your direct reports—who will be held responsible for the nonprofit's struggles and achievements.

The key players in your nonprofit are your senior management team comprising your direct reports. The importance of the positions they hold can either delay or accelerate your ability to execute your plans for your organization during your first year. Improving your nonprofit is your mandate. Failing to do so will poison your career.

Without a management team that makes your vision a reality, you will fail. Succeeding as a CEO is always a group effort. Thus building your team as soon as possible is your top priority. Given the responsibilities of running a nonprofit, the days, weeks, and months will breeze by. So how do you allocate the time necessary when you have so little of it for building your dream team? One of the objectives of Framework 1 is to create the strongest direct-report roster as fast as possible. You'll combine the abundant information you gather from your interviews with the profile of professionals you need. You can then go about determining which current team members have what it takes, which don't, whether the underperformers are capable of improving, and what kind of people you need to hire to replace the ones who have left on their own or through your actions. With your ideal senior management team in place, you will have taken a significant step—often the most important one—to restructure your nonprofit according to your design.

Make no mistake about it, terminating staff is never easy. It will adversely affect many people. Your decision will shake up the employees, members of their immediate family, the staff in their department, and you as a CEO, including your human side. Then there's pressure to get it right. If you don't terminate employees appropriately, you could be sued, which could cost you your job. Despite taking every possible step, including coordinating with board members and HR and offering a generous severance package (if applicable), I've had disgruntled ex-employees still turn around and lawyer up. Welcome to life in the litigious modern world where nearly anyone can find an attorney! But your ability to make great decisions under pressure, including under threat of lawsuit, is one reason you were hired. Your willingness to take on such enormous responsibility, combined with the thrill of being at the helm of large-scale success, is what separates your professional drive from that of those who always seek safety over relentless career advancement.

At the same time, I never entered the position with the mindset that I needed to clean house by getting rid of people. Ripping and gripping through my employee directory has never been my plan. In fact, in my three CEO posts, three out of five direct reports made the transition into my new administration in my first twelve months as the new CEO. The other two out of five were a mix of people our organization had let go or staff that left on their own.

In Framework 1, you learned questions to ask your direct reports during one-on-one meetings. I typically gave my department heads seven days to provide their answers. Reviewing their written replies, I evaluated their writing skill and style. During our one-on-one meetings, I observed their answers to my questions, which I used to assess their verbal communication skills. Through both what they wrote and what they said, I was able to evaluate their level of competence. These provided me important preliminary assessments regarding their ability to lead their departments.

Without delay, you must measure each direct report's leadership and, in particular, the role he or she will play in your plan for the nonprofit. Ask yourself:

1. How will each senior leader help me implement my ambitious vision?
2. Do I maintain or terminate an employee, rebuild or restructure my senior leadership team to push my vision across the finish line?

During the hiring process, you expressed your vision for the nonprofit. Part of the compelling case you made motivated the hiring committee to appoint you to fill the nonprofit's top executive role. They believed you would wholeheartedly and doggedly execute your exceptional plan. Your inspiring sales pitch won you the job. Now that you're in this important post, how do you make your actions speak louder than your words?

Are You an Insider or Outsider CEO?

AS YOU RECALL FROM FRAMEWORK 1, insider CEOs are promoted internally to lead the nonprofit, and outsider CEOs have never worked for the organization. Due to their history with the nonprofit, insider CEOs must often make a transition from being a peer with team members to being their appointed leader. This requires the insider CEO to shed the former colleague identity and take on one similar to that of an outsider CEO. Doing so is necessary to be able to take a fresh look at the nonprofit, including objectively evaluating the management team. Insider CEOs must be able to take an unabashedly unbiased look at former peers and determine whether they're capable of executing their new leader's vision.

I've had my colleagues who were hired as insider CEOs ask me what to do about specific challenges they faced. They were optimistic that a peer now turned direct report would be onboard with their plan.

"Brian, I'm all for the one-on-one meetings you recommend. But I already know certain direct reports really well. So I can save a lot of time by skipping them."

I always insisted that they stick to my plan.

"Just because you worked together as direct reports in the past doesn't mean you know how they ran their department and the processes, background information, and people they used to carry out their duties," I replied.

As an insider CEO, you must understand all departments and the people in them far beyond what was previously the case.

Unfortunately, your direct reports may continue to see you as their fellow direct report and not their boss. While you may masterfully make this transition, your colleagues may not. This is one reason why most boards hire outsider CEOs. Some insider CEOs initially hesitated following my advice but did so anyway. They often told me how amazed they were in what they learned about their direct reports after their one-on-one meetings.

"We've worked together for years, so I thought I knew everything I needed. Boy, was I wrong!" I've been told

In particular, these CEOs didn't know the precise motives behind past decisions their direct reports had made. The new leaders were glad they found out this and other information sooner than later. Sometimes they discovered, in order to perform the nonprofit's mission-critical work, which employees needed to be terminated.

Inside or outside CEO, your job is to evaluate who will stay and who has to go. If you delay, you run the risk of experiencing abject career failure. Sometimes employees leave on their own, which saves you from being the bad guy. Some see the changes required of them, and they refuse to adapt for multiple reasons. They may believe they aren't capable of making the transition, they may not agree with what you're requiring of them, they may like the former CEO and don't like you, or they may not be interested in executing what you expect of them. Whether you or the employee is doing the elimination, you're still left to fill the position. With one

CEO I replaced, some of his direct reports followed him. To my relief, the exodus had nothing to do with me. They were loyal to their boss and wanted to stick with him. But filling so many mission-critical positions quickly was no small feat! With my clear restructuring plan in place, I had a guide to inform my hiring decisions.

Your Executive Assistant and Your Talent Assessment

YOUR TRUSTED EXECUTIVE ASSISTANTS are your secret talent assessment weapons. An EA that has served in that capacity for years likely knows far more about the nonprofit than the newly appointed CEO. When you think about EAs, they are the eyes and ears of the nonprofit's leader. They managed the calendar of the previous CEO, sat in meetings where important decisions were made, and know the key players in and outside the organization.

With the EAs I worked with when I was CEO of nonprofits, the early trust we built gave me key insight about the nonprofit's history, including prior decisions and actions made and the motives behind them. Because I had been selected as the person that had the passion and commitment needed to make changes within the nonprofit, the EAs knew that I needed their support. They also understood the Search Committee tacitly required them to play a role in executing my plan.

As far as moving through Framework 1 was concerned, EAs played a central role in my effort to learn about the nonprofit and the community via my intense series of meetings you've read about. My EAs scheduled my appointments and performed research I needed. Through our close collaboration, they provided their perspective regarding the talent of the team I inherited based on their history with these individuals. I received background about board members and staff. The EAs described the strengths and weaknesses of the previous CEOs they had worked under. This helped me identify possibly difficult and inefficient people and processes and how I would address them. I discovered problems the previous CEO knew needed to be solved but was unwilling to do so. It was now my job to put out these fires.

The information I received was useful to fulfill my pledge to the nonprofit. I would take these preliminary insights from my EAs and then go about verifying them during my meetings that are part of Framework 1.

One EA told me how a direct report was a task master. "Lori's known around here to be really tough on her employees and even intimidating," my EA said.

I went into my one-on-one meeting with Lori with that information in mind. During our conversation, she described how she had two people in her department under performance-improvement plans. "I really want the best for them, so I'm willing to provide whatever support they need," she said.

Lori described the steps she was taking to make sure her staff knew exactly what was expected of them. This included sitting them down in one-on-one meetings, completing a performance review plan, and working with HR.

"So much for being an intimidating taskmaster," I thought to myself. "Lori's doing her utmost to be as professional and helpful as possible to her underperforming staff members."

My meeting with Lori reinforced why combining my EA's observations with my own investigation was a wise decision.

While I didn't use all the background my EAs provided, I was fortunate that many of their insights gave me information to consider and played a role in helping me make decisions based on solid facts. As you move through Framework 1, it's as if you're taking a drink from a firehose. Being overwhelmed by so many tasks is all too easy. The information EAs provided me beforehand offered an additional perspective before meeting people for the first time. I appreciated how they gave me some understanding of the direct reports' history with the nonprofit.

Working with my EAs gave me additional insight into the capabilities of employees—including me. I quickly learned that talent assessment goes both ways; my EAs evaluated my performance, and I tapped them for their opinions about me. Through our close work together, they observed how I was active and engaged inside and outside the nonprofit and a positive force for change. Sold on what I planned and excited to be part of writing this new chapter for the nonprofit, they were my early cheerleaders and advocates. Board members knew EAs were powerful sources of preliminary information about newly appointed CEOs. So they used my EAs' perspectives as one way to assess my performance. My EAs would tell me about being asked questions such as, "How's Brian doing?" "How's it working with him?" "What does he have you working on?" and "What's he been up to since the last time I visited the office?"

Often, after several weeks had passed since they had last met with me or were in the office, they wanted an update from the EA. Specifically, they sought his or her status update and perspective on my leadership. They also probed to see if the EA was on board and energized with my plan and satisfied working with me.

My wife, Liz, was the first person to hear about the plans I was most excited about. And my EAs were second. By knowing about my vision, they were able to help me execute it. They were also charged to keep my plans confidential. I've heard stories of EAs leaking information and thereby breaching confidentiality and thwarting a CEO's plans. Fortunately, my EAs always passed the mole test and maintained the healthy trust we built necessary to uphold the highest professional standards. Receiving my EAs' opinions and observations served as one data point among many I used to evaluate my direct reports. Before one-on-one meetings, my EAs provided background information about the direct reports. Afterward, I often ran by what I learned with my EAs. I appreciated that they verified or provided a different account of what I had been told.

In the event that I was responsible to apply my talent assessment process to hire an EA, the search always took several months because my needs were specific and required an exceptionally skilled person to fill the role. Spending time and money to ensure I found the right EA was worth every minute and dollar. Furthermore, I received help from other departments, including my direct reports and their EAs. Doing so served three purposes: my search was made easier, I had an opportunity to work closely with my management team, and I saw who was eager to support the new boss.

Your Board and Your Talent Assessment

IN ADDITION TO YOUR EA, your board members are an important source for assessing your team's quality. Thus building trust is critical. You will receive input from many people in and outside your nonprofit, but the most important voices are those of your board. In particular, your board officers and Executive Committee members have worked closely with your direct reports. In every assignment, the board chair or Executive Committee member gave me a read-between-the-lines warning: They were considering making senior staff changes before I was hired. But they held off and waited until I was CEO because they wanted the decision left to me. This was an indirect way to point out to me difficult team members that I needed to pay close attention to. I would compare this information with what I gathered from my one-on-one meetings and come to my own conclusions. Sometimes board officers disclosed this information as a test to see how willing I was to make staff shakeups to benefit the nonprofit.

If board officers brought to my attention problematic staff, I then went about confirming what I was told. I first spoke with HR to see if it had any concerns about this person. Then I reviewed the individual's file. I also observed how this person interacted with colleagues and staff. If the complaints and what I witnessed corroborated with the officers' account, this signaled that it was time to have a frank and confidential discussion with the employee. Now it was my task to give the direct reports the opportunity and resources to improve. In most instances, they didn't. Resisting change is part of human nature because the status quo is familiar, easy, and safe and change can be frightening. In this case, I needed to take the difficult steps of terminating the employee.

When staff left, whether by my prompting or on their own, I always let my board know right away. This is one instance of how I always upheld clear communication with my board. Doing so also prevented inaccurate office gossip from spreading about the person's departure.

Talent Assessment Is in Your Hands

AS THE NEW CEO, you are the only one responsible to shake up your direct report lineup. Through your one-on-one meetings, you may have identified weaknesses within some team members that signal you need to terminate people. Most likely, their staff or colleagues or both have recognized similar faults and thus would agree with your assessment.

Despite entering my position without intending to eliminate any positions, during my three CEO assignments, I always made staff changes, including dismissing people. Inevitable workplace dynamics common in all nonprofits, coupled with your specific goals, mean you'll most likely find yourself doing the same.

Because every leader has a different vision for his or her nonprofit, the direct report characteristics that raise red flags are specific to you. At the same time, certain cues team members give you are universal throughout all organizations. The following are the top-ten examples I encountered. While I hope otherwise for you, inevitably you'll hear similar statements during your one-on-one meetings and afterward. As you read these sometimes downright distasteful comments, consider how you would respond to them and the role they will play in your talent assessment.

The Rude, the Bad, and the Ugly List

1. I applied for your position, but you got it because the board thinks I am not good enough. But I know otherwise.
2. I've been here over twenty years, and I will let you know if I will stay or go, given what you want to do as our CEO.
3. If you want to remain in your position, you'd better know how to raise money or don't plan on being here very long. If you don't believe me, talk to the guy you replaced.
4. I am friends with a lot of people on the board . . . just in case you're thinking about making any changes in my area.
5. One of our largest donors has his name on the building. So if you're going to recommend shutting down programs or the building that has his name on it, good luck.
6. I have a personal relationship with a board member who's also a generous donor. She provides us plenty of support to my area, so you can just stay away from my department.
7. I have some information on employees who are doing unethical things, but I'm not comfortable telling you who they are and what they're up to.
8. My plan is to hang on for three more years until my wife retires, and then I'm done.
9. I think you should fire Sara because she's just not our kind of team member.
10. I heard there was a special audit performed. This doesn't sound good . . . but I don't know what was found.

Sometimes the motive behind some of these downright provocations is to test the new CEO, similar to the infamous hazing rituals in college Greek life. I never engaged in these power games staff played to establish their ground or top-dog status. In fact, they typically caused me to lose respect for the direct report. You have to use your judgment to determine when you'll defend yourself and stand your ground and when you'll step back and say nothing. In either case, you'll take note of the harsh words and determine the role they'll play in your assessment of your senior leader.

Even in instances of initial bad behavior on the part of my direct reports, I always gave them the benefit of the doubt . . . this is my approach to my personal and professional lives. While a blunt statement early on usually isn't grounds for letting people go, it certainly can play a role in evaluating them and contributes to building a case against them later on if they consistently obstruct your leadership authority.

I always followed the guidelines to document and meet with people to lay out my expectations. If they could not perform to the standard expected of them, they needed to go. They might have been opposed to my decision, but in the end, I'm the one who would be held responsible for the nonprofit's performance.

Briefing Board Members When Terminating Leaders

I ALWAYS GAVE MYSELF EIGHTEEN MONTHS at most to build my ideal senior management team. Working at a fast pace and factoring in the careful and often slow process of making sure my decisions were protecting the nonprofit in the event that I needed to terminate an employee, about a year and a half was a reasonable timeframe. I strived for sooner but kept eighteen months as a goal. When termination was necessary, I always did my best to keep my board leadership abreast of my plans. Specifically, I maintained clear communication lines with the board chair and vice chair, who were the people I directly reported to. The board chair and vice chair also served as a supportive sounding board. Informing them wasn't required, but their support would strengthen my case in the event that other board members or donors disagreed with my decision. While this preemptive action I took was wise and I recommend you follow it, I never had board leadership go against my decision. In fact, 99 percent of the time, I was fully supported.

I recall once a board member told me, "We don't want to fire Regina. She's been here a long time. That's your decision." In other words, they hired me as CEO, and they wanted me to play bad cop. After I performed my own assessment, I determined she needed to go. Afterward, the board member thanked me.

"What a relief, Brian! We've been waiting for someone to finally take action, and we're glad you did it," I was told.

As far as legal compliance is concerned, always consult an HR professional or employment attorney to make sure you've taken the steps to protect you and your nonprofit (such as maintaining the proper paper trail and keeping your board chair abreast of your actions). In the event of a lawsuit, your goal is to have a watertight case.

Once you've taken the appropriate steps to terminate a person, including following the recommendations of experts, consulting with your board, and thoroughly documenting your case, let go of doubt and be confident you're taking action based on objectivity, doing what's best for your nonprofit's long-term interests, and fulfilling your promise to the hiring committee.

Accountability and Assessing Your Team's Accomplishments

IMAGINE THAT AFTER IMMENSE TIME, energy, and resources, you've finally built your dream senior management team. Your direct reports could have all the best intentions in the world. But the work you all do is a big waste of time without a system in place to track you and your team's performances and the major changes you're making.

As CEO, your responsibility is to have a process to hold yourself and your management team accountable. A solid tracking system will require you to have a clear vision of where you'll take your nonprofit. Armed with this powerful plan developed from a place of unwavering clarity, you'll be able to effectively lead your team. Taking another step back, you can build a truly great team only if you know exactly what you're looking for. Without a precise vision of whom you need to fill your bench, your dream team may be nothing more than a delusion of greatness. Thus your tracking system is also your recruiting tool.

Frameworks 1 and 2 work together. You'll apply the information you gather in Framework 1 to Framework 2. As a result of following the first Framework, you've heard about your nonprofit from people inside and outside your organization. They've described their opinions about people, processes, and policies. This is all immensely useful information only if you use it to advance your plan. Without a clear process to measure the progress your nonprofit is making toward your goal, as well as keep your team accountable, months will go by without any tangible result to demonstrate your accomplishments. From small to big goals, each one must have clear benchmarks that determine whether they've been reached.

If you're meeting your goals, great. Your ambition and quest for excellence will mean you'll set even more ambitious ones. If, on the other hand, you're coming up short, then this is valuable information you'll use to determine what changes you need to make to put you on the path of high achievement. These changes often involve your team. You must ask yourself how daring and bold you're willing to be to establish the vision you were hired to execute, including restructuring and rebuilding your management team. This last point is when your commitment is put to the test. Many have all the ambition in the world but immediately hit pause on their motivation when they see they must face adversity in order to realize their goals.

Key Talent Assessment Questions by Department

PRIOR TO YOUR APPOINTMENT AS CEO, you didn't work in every department within your nonprofit. Thus questions in this section are designed to quickly separate good from bad direct reports within departments inside and outside your expertise and experience.

They are intended to be answered by you and your HR Department head first. I always worked closely with my HR leader when it came to assessing the talent of, terminating, or hiring direct reports, so I directed the questions I deemed appropriate to him or her. Then, if I sought answers from direct reports, I met with them to outline my specific questions and requested that all replies be emailed back to me for review. I let them know that if I required additional clarification for their answers, I would request a follow-up one-on-one meeting.

As you review the following questions, make sure you collect as much data as possible for each one. You'll use this, along with the talent assessment you performed during your one-on-one meetings, to make hiring or terminating decisions. These answers provide objective information you'll use with subjective information via your interactions with your direct reports to perform your talent assessment.

HR Direct Report Questions about Other Departments

- How often is the HR leader called upon to assist senior leadership team members and their departments with personnel issues?
- Do the data show concerns the HR department head has of any particular department? *Items of concern might be the frequency of turnover in a department, calls and concerns from employees, any potential legal concerns of items not being addressed, or legal issues the organization is currently facing that you as the new CEO should be aware, etc.*
- Does the organization follow a compensation schedule or salary scale showing jobs and the level of compensation from high to low for each position? *Having*

a salary structure is a key part of controlling costs and planning. It eliminates discretionary increases by management, provides transparency, and shows the organizational hierarchy. The openness and organizational chart are reassuring and motivating for employees because the information assures them of being paid fairly compared to their peers and provides a clear career ladder. Having a pay structure reduces awkwardness between managers and employees. It also keeps the organization in line with market-based salaries.

- When was the last time salary scales for each position were reviewed and updated? *Having these categories and salary scales regularly updated assures that pay is fair and that management can be confident individuals performing the same job duties are being treated in an equitable way. There is not a whole lot of room to play favorites or to have unfair pay treatment. In addition, new hires will have an assigned grade and be brought on based on a salary consistent with their experience and education level for the position.*
- What department in the organization requires the most time and effort from HR?
- What guidance is most frequently provided by the HR leader to various leaders in the organization?
- Is the person running the HR Department certified? *Having a certified HR leader is a key link between management and the employee workforce to make solid hiring decisions, along with appropriate policies and procedures. While my intent is not to endorse any specific HR certification, I always look for some certification as a reliable means to measure proficiency. All the excellent*

HR directors I've hired had the prerequisite educational background, experience, and HR certification.
- What are the education levels and backgrounds of other people within the HR Department? *Key to having an effective plan and strategy for your organization is to have qualified professionals in this area. Different departments have different skills sets, and an HR leader with knowledgeable team members can assist a CEO and the organization to create and implement a proper compensation and benefits structure for the organization.*
- If nothing has been added to improve the organization such as payroll processing, tracking for the Affordable Care Act, an Employee Assistance Program, or other important items, have any been considered? Were there discussions regarding these concerns with past or current leadership before your arrival? Were they with board members? Senior staff? Both?
- Is there any onboarding of new employees by the HR Department? *Onboarding is immersing a new employee into the organization. It ensures a consistent message for every new employee and engages new hires to feel they are part of a winning team and the organization is committed to their future success.*
- Does each department provide onboard training for its new people, or is there an organizational strategy? Please explain.
- What types of training does the organization provide or invest in for the employees of the organization? Please explain.
- Is there an annual evaluation process? How is it conducted? Is it different for each department?

- How does the HR leader rate the senior leadership in each department? This assessment is obviously confidential to you as the new leader, and you should make that known in a direct conversation with your HR leader.

HR Direct Report Questions about All Departments

- What tools have been added to track key metrics for the organization?
- What problems keep the direct report up at night?
- What are the education levels and backgrounds of other people within this department?
- Do some jobs in the organization require certain levels of education or certification? If so, what are those positions?
- Who are the up-and-coming performers in this department? Who are the go-to people in this department?
- Did the direct report put together the current team of people in this department? If so, what is the history of how the team came together?
- If the direct report is not the person who put the current department together, what is the history of how the team came together?
- How would you rate this team?
- What personnel issues have there been in this department?
- What problems has this department had with other departments or people in the organization?
- Are these problems still being solved? Are these more personality or operating types of challenges the direct report faces?

- What is the biggest challenge the direct report faces from a talent perspective in his or her department?
- How would you or the direct report or both rate each member of his or her team? Do annual performance evaluations reflect your rating?

Go with Your Gut and Measure Your Progress

A BIG PART OF TALENT ASSESSMENT is trusting your CEO instincts. Once you perform your objective analysis, you then ask yourself, "Is this direct report a good match for the nonprofit and my vision for it?" Your senior managers could have all the right credentials in the world. But if you can't connect with them and can't see yourself working closely with them on day-to-day mission-critical projects, then it's time to take a hard look at whether they should stay or go.

Subjective analysis is not something a textbook or predictive index score can do for you. It comes from the expertise and skill set that brought you to where you are in your career today. I always considered objective and subjective information before making any termination or hiring decision.

Last, having a system in place to track the work you're performing and the major changes you're making is critical to holding yourself and your management team accountable. This system will measure the quality of decisions you've made as CEO. The process of creating a solid tracking system will require you to have a clear vision of where you plan to take the nonprofit. Armed with this powerful vision developed from a place of unwavering clarity, you'll be able to effectively lead your team.

Chapter 10

Framework 3: The Financials

> **In this chapter, you'll learn:**
>
> - how to analyze the numbers like a pro—even if you don't like numbers;
> - what your nonprofit's financial history can tell you;
> - the work auditors do and why their expertise matters to your nonprofit;
> - the importance of the chair of the Finance Committee;
> - what to do when your CFO leaves;
> - specific questions to ask and documents to request to learn your Finance Department's structure, each team member's skill sets, and their responsibilities.

Scott phoned me one day in a panic. He had recently been appointed CEO and needed help.

"My CFO handed me a stack of financial reports that he and his team put together when closing the books for the month. I just found out I need to work with him to provide a summary of the reports at the board meeting," he told me. "In my past role on the senior management team, I've never had to take such an in-depth look at these financial reports I have been asked to review. I don't know where to start with analyzing all this information or what follow-up questions I need to ask my CFO."

As a CEO, Scott would never reveal potentially credibility-crushing concerns and insecurities like this to anyone inside his nonprofit . . . let alone to his board. But like Scott, my other CEO colleagues know they can be honest and forthcoming with me. During our call, I gave him step-by-step instructions on how to analyze the data he received, who in his nonprofit could provide him guidance and information, and the questions he needed to ask.

For CEOs that don't like numbers, taking a deep dive into your nonprofit's finances is cumbersome, overwhelming, or even intimidating. But without solid understanding of financial analysis, you will not be able to achieve leadership excellence.

Whether we're in school or the workplace, number crunching and bean counters are often perceived as downright dull. That's an unfortunate bias we have in our society and one reason why I think a nonprofit's Finance Department is often not given the recognition it deserves.

Without this department, employees would not be paid or reimbursed, utility bills wouldn't be covered, expenses would exceed revenue and thus threaten the organization's viability, late payments to vendors would result in penalty fees or non-delivery of goods, and big donors wouldn't be able to see proof of the nonprofit's fiscal health.

In this chapter, we'll give finance and the Finance Department the acknowledgment they deserve. I'll provide you the basics you need to know from day one when it comes to your nonprofit's finances, including information you need to uncover and questions you need to ask. Be assured that what you'll learn is accessible and clear to any leader who seeks to be well rounded, which is an important part of how you'll continually ascend the leadership ladder.

Working with nonprofit CEOs, I've found that the weak spot for many is finance. Prior to being appointed head of their organizations, most professionals have had to focus only on their department. They have been charged to put together a budget and be responsible to make sure their team stays within their expense lines on an annual basis. For me, I was fortunate to have been a senior budget analyst prior to transitioning to the nonprofit sector.

When I was earning my graduate degree at the University of Chicago, I took a budgeting course for public and nonprofit agencies. My professor told me:

> *If you want to be an exceptional executive, begin your career working in a budget shop in a local or state government setting. You'll learn how to crunch numbers and become analytical in how you interpret legislation that affects the programs government departments fund. Your recommendations can change the course of the funding of programs.*

At the time, I questioned if I wanted to go down the path of being a number cruncher after earning my master's. But I trusted his judgment, and his advice made sense. Thus I interviewed for the position of budget analyst for the Bureau of the Budget with the state of Illinois. I was hired, and after graduating, I worked on the governor's staff reviewing and analyzing

Health and Human Services Department program budgets for the state. There, I gained invaluable experience in financial analysis. I learned the importance of budgeting and finance, which helped me become a successful fundraiser when I later moved to the nonprofit sector. There, I used my financial background to write and request support from individual donors, foundations, and government entities.

Once I became a CEO, I knew that for me to realize my plan for the nonprofit, I needed to first have a well-informed financial starting point. Thus I used my financial background to analyze numbers on a deeper level to evaluate the nonprofit's fiscal state at the beginning of my tenure.

Knowing the fiscal story of what took place prior to your appointment is important because it shows how the previous leader ran the organization. Like a detective, your investigation will uncover what went right and wrong. Questions you'll answer include:

- What revenues and expenses rose or fell?
- What did the twelve-month cash flow statement look like for the organization during the prior year?
- What did the monthly accounts receivable report show for outstanding payments on pledges to the organization?
- How was your nonprofit meeting its obligations in making payments to others, which would be reflected in the accounts payable report?

From your evaluation, you'll determine the weaknesses you need to fix and strengths you'll build on. In the future, when you complete your tenure as CEO, you too will leave your financial legacy. The numbers the next leader will analyze will show if you left your organization in better shape than when you arrived.

To perform your initial analysis well, you'll work with your Finance Department direct report, who is often a CFO. He or she has a wealth of information about your nonprofit and should be your trusted advisor. While this person may have a different designation, for the sake of simplicity throughout this chapter, I'll refer to him or her as CFO. While you're a CEO and not a CFO, to run your organization well, you'll be responsible to make important financial decisions. To do so successfully, you need to know what financial questions to ask, the implications of the various answers, and specific accounting information regarding whatever problem you're charged to solve, programs you seek to fund, or direction you plan to take your nonprofit, such as shrinking it when the broader economy slumps or expanding it during boom times. Thus a solid understanding of your nonprofit's finances is essential for you to successfully lead.

Your Nonprofit's Monthly Closing of Books

From your CFO, you'll receive audit results and annual reports. This is a basic step, and from here, you'll need to dig deeper. You need to compare your nonprofit's current budget with its actual performance on a monthly basis. You'll find this information in your nonprofit's monthly closing of the books that your CFO will provide to you.

In the back of my mind throughout this process, I always asked myself, "Are we meeting our budget revenue projections? If not, how would we make up the difference to meet them?"

Each month, the CFO and his or her team organized the closing of books and sent it to me. I combed through it, and if I needed clarification or had a question, the CFO and I worked together to resolve all issues.

As CEO, it was my job, along with the CFO's, to add comments when needed in any board meeting pertaining to our finances. I always appreciated this aspect of the job because it gave us a chance to tell our story and address concerns early on through the numbers we were presenting. By directly communicating with the board and answering their questions, I avoided the fallout (sometimes out of control) that often takes place once the rumor mill starts churning. The best way to avoid the consequences of the rumor mill is to make sure it doesn't start!

For example, we had projected a certain amount of revenue to come in for a particular month. If the money showed up earlier than planned, then I looked forward to sharing the good news that we were ahead of our projection. Or if revenue didn't come in as projected but would be arriving next month, I let the board know about the delay and provided reassurance about the late timing. Or if we were not meeting our budget revenue projections, I let them know I had requested that the resource development team or the Finance Department tell me why we had not received the funding as projected, and I would update the board once I received answers.

Also, after decades of running nonprofits, I observed that accounting rules for nonprofit organizations change nearly every other year. So make sure your CFO stays up-to-date on such changes. Your auditors will also inform your CFO of such changes, particularly when they come to perform the annual audits of your organization.

After my CFO and I agreed on the monthly closing reports and were ready to present it at the monthly board meeting, we forwarded it to the finance chair. This board member sits on the board's Executive Committee, oversees the board's Finance Committee, and presents the report at board meetings. (All high-performing nonprofits have a finance chair that works closely with the CFO and CEO.) This person combed through the various income statements and budget reports to be presented. If the finance chair needed clarification or had questions, he or she presented them to the CFO and CEO and received answers from us.

Now, we had a thoroughly vetted monthly report ready to present to the full board for its approval. These prior steps were the dress rehearsal for the debut performances. The finance chair then presented the final report during board and Executive Committee meetings. This action was recorded in meeting minutes, which is an important step to fulfill oversight, compliance, fiduciary duties, and auditing requirements for the nonprofit.

Auditors and Yearly Closing of Books

FOR YOUR NONPROFIT TO RUN WELL and attract the best donors and volunteers, it must be evaluated in the most objective, rigorous, independent, and transparent way possible.

An independent audit is an examination of your accounting records and financial statements by a third-party auditor, who is a certified public accountant (CPA). Your nonprofit hires auditors to perform this work. They conduct an independent investigation into your nonprofit's financial record keeping. The IRS does not require nonprofits to conduct audits. But many states mandate nonprofits to submit a copy of audited financial statements when they register as a charitable nonprofit. This process is called a charitable registration, which is how states authorize nonprofits to engage in fundraising activities. Also, some donors require an audited financial statement from the nonprofit to qualify for funding. Many banks and other potential lenders require the same from nonprofits.

Some states also specify that nonprofits receiving public funding submit independent audits to the state agency that provided the funding for a particular program that year. If a nonprofit receives any government funds—state or federal—I always recommend determining whether the state or federal entity has an accompanying audit requirement beyond your annual independent audit.

In addition, Uncle Sam requires nonprofits to conduct an independent audit if the nonprofit receives more than $750,000 in federal funds for a single year. In other words, in addition to your organization's independent annual audit, your nonprofit is required to perform a separate single audit of the program the federal government funded. This was the case during several of my CEO assignments. Thanks to the diligence of my CFO and Finance Department, we were always in full compliance with the state and federal governments.

While taking a deep dive into the audit process, which is complicated, technical, and essential to your nonprofit's success, is beyond the scope of this chapter, my advice for you is to work closely with your CFO. Specifically, upon the start of your tenure, have a series of in-depth, one-on-one meetings with him or her to understand the types of audits being conducted within your nonprofit. You want to know when and how many audits will take place, their deadlines, if any will be required outside the annual independent audit, and how much time you and your staff will need to complete these reviews with each auditor.

Finally, if your nonprofit is a part of a national organization or federation, your nonprofit will be required to perform an annual independent audit to satisfy the membership standards. Furthermore, the national organization and its board must approve the audit findings for your nonprofit to be declared in good membership standing.

After auditors review all management and financial information, they prepare the audit report that will be presented to the nonprofit's Audit Committee. Auditors work with the CFO and the Finance Department. This often entails specific questions directed to the CEO and relevant members of the senior management team. Thus the CEO and CFO *cooperate* with the auditors but do not direct its findings or outcome. Instead, part of the audit evaluates the CEO, CFO, and management team's actions that produced the results for that year. In order to uphold third-party independence, the CEO, CFO, and Audit Committee, which is a subgroup of the board, are not part of producing the audit report.

Rather, auditors present their findings to the Audit Committee. Each year, the board's Nominating Committee appoints the Audit Committee's chair, as it does with the leaders of all the committees and which the board votes to approve.

The Audit Committee oversees and ultimately approves the audit report, which is then presented to the board for its full approval.

Together with the auditors, the Audit Committee reviews the organization's financial performance over the prior year. The comments auditors provide in their report and review will give the public information about the nonprofit's performance. In addition, auditors identify strengths and weaknesses within the nonprofit they have found during their review. This helps the organization improve its work internally and serves as a guide as to what the organization and its Finance Department will work on during the current fiscal year to improve any deficiencies the audit pointed out.

Auditors perform the following tasks:

- Review the nonprofit's accounting and recording procedures
- Review written meeting minutes of the board and Executive Committee meetings
- Evaluate financial reports presented at all board meetings
- Analyze all the organization's accounts and transactions
- Examine how transactions are processed for payroll, health benefits, and many other items that take place over the course of the fiscal year
- Review how the financial staff recorded gifts and grants made to the nonprofit to determine if they were properly documented
- Interview the CEO, CFO, HR senior leader, board, finance chair, other members of the senior leadership team, and even contributors to verify pledges made if they have not yet been fulfilled
- Determine if there are any legal matters that may affect the financial health of the organization if a legal action is pending

- Identify if there is coverage of a legal matter if the organization did not win the suit and if there is insurance to cover a pending legal matter

If the nonprofit books a grant or gift as revenue, the auditors will do the following:

- Determine if the grant or gift was restricted or unrestricted to the nonprofit
- Request a copy of the grant or gift document that details what the organization is expected to do with the funds once they are received from the grantor
- Verify if it was recorded correctly
- Ask questions regarding every aspect of the grant or gift such as if it spans one or more years
- Ask whether it will be recorded as revenue for one fiscal year or over a multi-year period (multi-year agreements require specific documentation)
- Make sure the grant or gift money already secured is being used as specified by the grant
- Review any reports the granting organization submitted such as final reports verifying how the nonprofit spent funds

Because volunteers govern nonprofits, you're responsible to make sure your nonprofit, board officers, and committees uphold the highest and clearest transparency standards. The credibility you build with your donors is key to continuing to receive their generous support. Keep in mind that individual donors, foundations, and other entities providing money to the nonprofit can request a copy of the annual audit report.

I always offered to share my nonprofit's audit with donors if they had not seen it because it gave them an opportunity to review a third-party evaluation of my organization's fiscal and business practices for the prior year. In addition, I directed and encouraged donors to look my nonprofit up in Charity Navigator, which is a nonprofit rating and review site. One of its evaluation criteria is nonprofits posting their audits online. You do want the public to be able to review your audits from your website, including the auditor's full report, which contains its comments about the organization's fiscal health for the prior year.

Finding the Right Volunteer to Head the Finance Committee

THROUGHOUT MY TWENTY-FIVE-YEAR CAREER AS CEO of nonprofits, one of my top priorities regarding board talent assessment was to find the ideal volunteers to be a part of the Finance Committee and to find an individual board member to lead it.

From closing the monthly books to reporting at board meetings and working with auditors and the organization's Finance and Audit Committees, the responsibilities of a finance chair are significant and highly influential. It takes someone with the financial acumen to work with staff leadership to uphold the nonprofit's commitment to fiscal transparency and responsibility. Finance chairs play a key role in any high-achieving nonprofit.

One prerequisite I sought for a finance chair was someone working in an auditing firm or with a Certified Public

Accounting (CPA) designation or both. To become a CPA requires rigorous training and expertise that provides an extremely high financial oversight standard. CPAs are trained to uphold professional standards in the accounting industry. I always worked alongside CPA volunteers to review all financial information for every nonprofit I led. Specifically, because CPAs speak the auditing language at a highly sophisticated level, they're indispensable advisors to the CEO and CFO during reviews of the organization's financial performance.

In general, the auditing community is closely knit. Thus the auditors within one firm know others from competing firms. So having a finance chair who is a partner or part of one auditing firm review the work of the firm that performed your nonprofit's audit provides your nonprofit a second layer of rigorous accountability.

Once you start as the new leader, assess the level of volunteer talent you have on your Finance Committee. If a CPA isn't on your current roster, consider how you could find one. Start the recruiting process through the Nominating Committee, which comprises committee chairs of the board and often the CEO. In such a position, you as CEO can have a major influence over the board's composition, as well as future committee leaders and especially the finance chair, along with an audit chair. Thus I recommend CEOs provide input into the men and women they think the Nominating Committee should consider. Work with your board chair and vice chair as soon as possible to determine the succession plan for key people for these chair positions. This is a very important part of the partnership you wish to build with your board leadership.

Your first year, however, you most likely are learning about your board. During this time, you'll count on the judgment of your current board to determine which members will lead these committees.

Framework 1 provides you the tools to work with your board quickly and effectively once you begin your tenure. As a result, you'll be able to play a more significant role in your Nominating Committee's decisions faster than otherwise possible. As you evolve in your role rapidly thanks to following Framework 1, you'll determine if your current finance chair has what it takes to fulfill your vision. This is the benefit of thoroughly knowing your finance chair's roles, responsibilities, and job descriptions. To effectively perform their role, finance chairs must have the necessary prerequisite skills such as a CPA designation, degree, and years of experience.

Unless you precisely identify what you need, you'll be basing your search on mostly opinion and subjective criteria. If, after objective analysis, you need someone with better credentials and expertise than the person currently filling the finance chair post, first bring your concerns up to the board chair. Work with him or her to determine who will replace your current finance chair. Once you find your ideal candidate, bring that person to serve on your board and committees as quickly as possible. As you learned in Framework 2, building your senior management dream team reflects your ability to lead well. By doing so, you're earning credibility within your community by showing you're heading a strong, viable operation. Similarly, a dream board demonstrates your nonprofit's strength.

When Your CFO Abruptly Departs

IMAGINE YOU WERE HIRED AS CEO and, after months of nonstop work, you've finally hit your stride. Suddenly, your CFO that you depended on tells you she needs to resign to take care of important family matters. You've worked closely with her from the start, and now you'll be overseeing the Finance Department as you work to find her replacement.

In Chapter 5, "Framework 1: One-on-One Meetings during Your First Ninety Days," I provided you checklists. These are examples of how CEOs must know the roles and responsibilities of each position in each department. After you've completed these checklists with your direct reports, you're able to evaluate if the Finance Department's second in command is prepared to work alongside you during this time of change or even to replace the departing CFO.

During my CEO tenure, if I determined he or she was up to the task while we searched for a permanent replacement, I said, "We've lost our CFO and we will need to navigate together during this time of transition. I am counting on you to lead the finance team, and I will support you as we make our way through this time together. The best way for us to view our challenge is to use the mindset that our CFO is on vacation, which is how you have managed the department on those occasions."

I use the vacation imagery because when your boss is away and you're second in command, you're responsible to seamlessly run the department and keep its functions humming away. Because you know your supervisor's responsibilities, you fulfill them until he or she returns, which in this case is when a new CFO is hired.

Early in my career, I struggled with the in-between time when one CFO left and we had to fill the position. (In two instances, I avoided any struggle at all when I promoted the second in command to the direct report post.) What you read in Framework 1 is the culmination of how I learned to navigate this interim period effectively. I initially dreaded this in-between phase. But I eventually appreciated and actually enjoyed it because it provided me the opportunity to know the department team better, along with the work each person performed.

In addition, another benefit of well-qualified finance chairs is they most likely have gone through similar transitions in their workplaces. Thus they have a wealth of knowledge to help you through the process. Their experiences can lighten the burden you carry, and they are usually more than willing to pitch in to keep the department moving forward. In general, committee chairs of the board are vitally important to provide not only oversight but also expert advice when a change occurs that you didn't anticipate. This has happened to me several times. I've had to find a new CFO after my current one left due to retirement, moving away, illness, or finding a new job. Fortunately, I had the basic background necessary to navigate the department in the short-term until finding the right person to join our team or promote from within the organization.

Expanding Your Expertise

IN THEIR PREVIOUS POSITIONS, CEOs who weren't CFOs relied on the Finance Department for evaluating the financial performance of the department they oversaw. For example, a senior management team member of the Service Delivery and Program Department counted on the Finance Department to cover payroll and program funding. A resource development senior management team member worked with the Finance Department on accounts receivable and payable but not on closing the books monthly or cash flow analysis. Outsider CEOs coming from the private sector may have never dealt with nonprofit accounting, which follows different practices and rules than in the for-profit sector.

As CEO, you also must be familiar with your Finance Department's structure, along with each team member's skill sets and responsibilities. Before I headed nonprofits, I was a part of the senior leadership team that worked closely with my former bosses and volunteer leaders. In my role, I saw the importance of CEOs having a proper financial foundation from which they would lead. The absence of this skill set would hurt their credibility. Because these senior leaders understood this, they made good decisions after their CFOs unexpectedly stepped down. Board members and staff saw their competence because the CEOs had a plan of action in mind after losing this key staffer. They knew the functions of the people in the department, which illustrated they understood what needed to be taken care of, and asked for assistance from their finance chair and other board members.

Thankfully, I learned from them, and you can learn from me because I was fortunate to work for highly skilled CEOs and their leadership ability was an important part of my training. In the following checklists, you'll learn the questions to ask and the information to request that will show your staff, your board, and your community that you're prepared to fulfill the promises you made during your interview process.

I created these checklists after seeing the importance of being prepared for matters that may have been beyond my control. Over the course of my decades-long career, I documented practices that resulted in high achievement at the nonprofits I led. The checklists cover the following:

- Monthly financial preparation, analysis, and reporting
- Cash flow reporting and analysis
- Accounts payables reporting and analysis
- Accounts receivable reporting and analysis
- Annual operating budget and other budgeting requests
- Miscellaneous topics and analysis

Questions, Recommendations, and Requests of Documents from Your CFO

Monthly Financial Preparation, Analysis, and Reporting

- What schedule do the CFO and finance staff follow to close the books monthly for the organization?
- What statements and other reports are included in the financial packet presented to the board and Executive Committee? Request a copy and analysis of each item.

- Does the CEO review the financial packet from the CFO before it goes to the finance chair for the Finance Committee's review?
- Is the finance chair engaged and interested in reviewing these monthly statements? Does he or she thoroughly analyze the reports and ask the tough questions each month of the CFO and CEO?
- After their review of the financial packet, do the CFO and finance chair write a report to accompany it for presentation to the board?
- Do reports in the financial packet compare the budget to actual year-to-date (YTD) results? Do they also include the previous year's comparison of budget to YTD to indicate if deviations from the budget have occurred at this time before—and may call for refining the budget for this month next year?
- What other volunteer leaders review the financial packet or a part of it? When and why? Do they provide comments about it?
- Does the financial packet include descriptions of the activities taken place for the month? If so, they may provide information to pass on to the board. For example, if your nonprofit received a new grant that was not accounted for in the budget, you will highlight this great news to the board in a future meeting. When you do, you will most likely give it a heads-up that spending will increase because of the services your nonprofit is providing as a result of the new funding from the grant.
- Are the financials ready each month at the appropriate time for the board and Executive Committee meetings?

Note: All CFOs I've worked with have always had an excuse to explain why they couldn't close their books as quickly as they wanted or had planned. Common reasons include:

- "I haven't received the investment statements in the mail. Until I do, I can't close out revenue for this month."
- "I do not have enough finance staff to do the proper closing."
- "The Service Delivery Program Department has not given me the units of service, so I've been put behind on doing the monthly billing."

As your nonprofit's new leader, you must find out early on the Finance Department's prior performance in meeting or missing monthly deadlines. Next, be helpful! Identify the challenges it faces, and remove any roadblocks you can. Within one nonprofit I led, the timing of board and Executive Committee meetings caused the Finance Department to miss deadlines for submitting key reports. When I found this out, I took action with the board chair to move the date and time back a week. This allowed the Finance Department to have its reports completed on time.

In addition, I earned the department's appreciation. The previous CEO didn't bother figuring out the bottleneck that caused the delay, let alone alleviate it. My direct report was grateful I took the time to listen to her, figure out what was going wrong, and do my best to help. As you've learned throughout this book, asking questions is key to determining the strengths and weaknesses within your nonprofit and improving it.

While closing books on time is a challenge many nonprofit Finance Departments face, by remaining curious, eager to help, and optimistic, you may find solutions that your predecessors never did.

Cash Flow Reporting and Analysis

- Request a copy of the current monthly cash flow report.
- Request a monthly historical cash flow report reflecting the last three years.
- What does the analysis report indicate about the organization's cash flow?
- Is there a particular trend you see in the thirty-six-month report? Is it continuing into this year?
- Have your CFO describe to you the background and analysis of each cash flow report.
- According to your CFO, what contributed to positive cash flow over the past three-plus years?
- According to your CFO, what caused negative cash flow over that period?
- According to your CFO, in what months was cash flow a challenge and why?
- Confirm your CFO can talk to and describe all aspects of this report for you to understand.
- Who besides the Finance Department requests and reviews the cash flow report?
- Is there a daily cash flow report the CFO produces and provides to the CEO from the Finance Department? If not, request you start receiving one.

Accounts Payable Reporting and Analysis

- Request a copy of the most recent accounts payable (AP) report for the organization.
- What is the process for putting this report together? Who oversees the process? Who creates it? How often does it come out?
- Is there a weekly AP report developed by the CFO and the Finance Department? If an AP report is not prepared on a weekly basis, this delays payment of bills and knowing how much cash is needed to meet weekly obligations.
- If there is a weekly AP report, is there a meeting of key staff to decide what checks are processed for payment that week? Who makes these decisions of what gets paid and what payments will be delayed?
- If no such meeting or process takes place, who makes these decisions and how does the process take place? If no process is in place, does such a process need to be implemented?
- What is the policy for signing checks of the organization? How many signatures are required for each check? Is there a certain dollar amount that requires a board and senior staff signature?
- What are the policies regarding payments by the organization? For example, does the organization have thirty days to process an invoice from a vendor for payment? Is there a policy that no checks are processed unless the necessary documentation is attached to each invoice? Is that information attached for the signatories to review before signing?

- Do the CEO and CFO review the weekly AP report on a weekly basis to approve invoices for payment? If no, my recommendation is they should.
- Are restricted grants or program funds set aside to specifically pay for commitments in which they are intended? If no, I recommend they should be.
- How much does the organization require to make payroll each month?
- What type of report does the organization use to highlight weekly payable needs (including those weeks for payroll)? (Payroll is not usually on an AP report.) How does this tie into the weekly cash report?
- Most organizations are on a biweekly pay period (twenty-six a year). Is this the case for your organization? If no, what is the cycle?
- Can the CFO indicate if the organization has had challenges in meeting payroll for its employees? (If the CFO knows there are challenges to meeting payroll, to whom has he or she expressed any concerns? What actions have been taken to try to solve this problem?)
- Does the organization maintain a line of credit with a local financial institution?
- Has the organization used a line of credit over the last three years? If so, what were the circumstances to it being used? What was it used for and how much?
- What did you learn in reviewing the AP report provided to you?
- What will be your role in reviewing the AP process as the new CEO?

Accounts Receivable Reporting and Analysis

- Request a copy of the most recent accounts receivable (AR) report for the organization.
- Who in the Finance Department puts this report together?
- How does the Finance Department work with other staff regarding questions about the report's results?
- How often is the AR report updated and reviewed with key staff to collect on outstanding receivables?
- Who are the key people responsible for bringing in outstanding payments on these commitments?
- What has been the history of receivables not being collected in each of the last five years?
- How much is outstanding in the AR report? Does it track thirty-, sixty-, and ninety-day outstanding AR? If it does not track all three, I recommend that it do so.
- How much has been written off by the organization on commitments not being met by supporters?

Annual Operating Budget and Other Budgeting Requests

- How does the organization create the annual operating budget? Who in the Finance Department puts the annual operating budget together with the CFO? *The annual operating budget provides a reference point for the activities to be performed in the upcoming year by each department and the staff needed to carry out the activities. It also helps a CEO manage challenging financial periods when faced with unexpected expenses or crisis events. The questions of how the budget is created and who puts it together are important. You want to know if your direct reports and department leaders will take responsibility for their budget because they helped build it or if the finance department handed them the budget for them to manage.*

- How does the CFO and the finance staff interact with senior leadership to build the annual operating budget?
- What is your role as the CFO in the annual operating budget process? Does everything come in to you as the CFO from other departments? Or does it go to other people in your Finance Department? Please explain via a budget timeline and everything that goes into the process.
- How did the past CEO work with the CFO and the Finance Department to put together the annual operating budget?
- Are there any other types of budgets that must be formulated in tandem with the operating budget? Capital budgets? Budgets that must go to other funding agencies, which are a part of the annual operating budget? *These other budgets need to be understood regarding their revenues and expenses, but there is only one operating budget that guides the organization.*
- Are there different points in time during the fiscal year that affect the operating budget because other entities operate on a different fiscal year or budgeting cycle? This may include local and federal government funding, health benefits, and more.
- How would the CFO evaluate the skill level of the people in the Finance Department who report to him or her?

- Has the organization had any allegations of fraud or mishandling of funds? If so, were they before or during the current CFO's tenure in the Finance Department? What are the details?

Miscellaneous Topics and Analysis

- After reviewing these reports, the CEO and CFO should discuss the month's results. Even after the very thorough review to this point, issues always arise that may not clearly fall under any of these categories.
- A meeting between the current auditor and the CEO will provide more information that the CEO will share with others in the nonprofit.
- What additional information can volunteers who have been deeply involved with the finances of the organization provide to the CEO? For example, they might describe the background on why and how auditors, along with local financial institutions, were selected to furnish their services to the nonprofit. Or maybe they could describe the auditor selection process and which auditors weren't selected.
- How long have the auditors been auditing the books of the nonprofit? How long have they worked with the current CFO?
- Ask the auditors how they would characterize their work with the CFO and the Finance Department staff.
- Is the CFO happy with the work performed by the auditors on an annual basis?
- Are the auditors responsive and accessible to the CFO if they are needed during the course of the year?

- Other items not covered are requests of documents for any investment policies, endowments, and creation of trusts from others that benefit the financial health of the organization. If these documents exist, the CEO and CFO should review them. While they don't have to be reviewed immediately, if they do exist, the CEO should study them, including who created the policies and when and if the board has reviewed and approved them.
- What additional items should the CFO review with the new CEO?
- Have special funds been developed within the organization? If so, what are the details—for what purpose, for how much, under what terms?
- Does concern about an issue or process keep the CFO up at night? If so, how can this be addressed? Who in the organization should be consulted?

Summary

As you learned from Framework 1, there's no substitute for meeting with your direct reports and volunteers one-on-one. No amount of emails, texts, or even Zooms can replace the information you'll gather and the problems you'll solve from in-person casual conversations to intense, formal meetings. The same holds true for your nonprofit's finances. While the numbers themselves are critical, so too are your meetings with your CFO and Finance Department.

Working closely with this often-unheralded group of professionals is the only way that you will fulfill the promises you made when you were hired and that earned you the top position of the nonprofit.

The numbers and the team behind the number crunching tell one of the most significant stories detailing your nonprofit's strengths and weaknesses. The future of your nonprofit relies on its fiscal health, so your understanding of it is key to your success.

Chapter 11

Framework 4: Donor Relationships

In this chapter, you'll learn:

- how to distinguish between revenue sources versus donor development;
- effective strategies to evaluate your nonprofit's revenue portfolio in order to build upon its strengths, improve upon its weaknesses, and thus meet your goals;
- why you should have a Resource Development Department;
- how to assess individual line items of your nonprofit's income statement;
- to develop the powerful mindset that is key to establishing your leadership legacy.

IN THE WORLD OF PERSONAL FINANCE, you always hear money managers talk about the importance of a balanced portfolio to meet your income needs during your retirement. What *balanced* means depends on your circumstances. Assessing your present and future needs, income, expenses, and risks is a key part of how financial advisors design a healthy portfolio.

You play a similar role in your nonprofit. Evaluating its portfolio is a critical task to perform early in your tenure. In this case, your portfolio comprises your nonprofit's revenue, which you'll find in its income statement.

Your organization's portfolio is how it meets its most ambitious goals (which are ones you've envisioned), adapts to external challenges out of your control (such as inevitable economic downturns and unexpected catastrophes such as the coronavirus), and adeptly pivots when major funding sources disappear.

Nonprofit revenue is the cash generated through your fundraising activities and other sources. Fundraising activities include:

- Appeals to individuals and companies
- Events
- Charitable foundation and government grant solicitations
- Social media appeals to the public

Other sources include:

- Interest income from an annual endowment draw
- Quarterly or annual income from trusts and foundations held by others
- Fees charged for services your nonprofit provides to the community such as educational classes like CPR and first aid, parenting classes, and other training sessions related to your nonprofit's work
- Membership fees from clients who are part of your nonprofit's programs

- Fees generated from the sales of a product or merchandise fees from some other type of transactional event taking place that generates revenue for your organization

Keep in mind that the Resource Development Department is not a source of revenue. Its job is to build relationships with potential and current donors so they will give generously to your mission. Their contributions then fall into the "appeals to individuals and companies" above.

Each organization has its own revenue sources. Your job as the new CEO is to understand which department oversees annual revenue generation and activity in order to have a firm grasp on your revenue sources. In this chapter, you'll learn how to evaluate your nonprofit's revenue portfolio. By doing so, you'll identify its strengths and improve upon its weaknesses, which is critical to meeting your goals.

The Importance of Your Resource Development Department

As a CEO, one of my biggest responsibilities was to raise cold-hard cash for my nonprofit. The amount of money I generated was one of the main measures of my efficacy. If my nonprofit remained in the red, my days on the job would have been numbered. The opposite is true as well. My solid track record of generating revenue for my nonprofits is one of my proudest professional accomplishments.

No high-performing CEOs succeed on their own. Their achievements are a team effort. When it comes to fundraising,

I could have never met my biggest objectives without a stellar Resource Development Department, which comprised a team of staff and volunteers who had the right tools to do their work.

In two of my three assignments, I walked onto the job without having a Resource Development Department. Knowing this would make it impossible for me to meet my revenue targets, I had to convince my board leadership that the nonprofit needed this department to generate and increase revenue, which it would use to expand the work of the organization.

The common counterargument I heard was that the nonprofit was already writing grants, organizing special events, and successfully raising revenue in multiple other ways. Thus, a new department was unnecessary. To address this, I explained that one of the reasons the nonprofit hired me was to uncover additional revenue so it could expand the organization's programs and services.

A nonprofit's grant writer completes one grant and then moves on to the next, usually with no follow-up with grantors to learn how their grant dollars are being spent. Likewise, special event staff plan one event and then move on to the next without subsequently working to bring guests and their invitees closer to the nonprofit. The Resource Development Department overcomes these gaps in connection, often working with the grant writer and event and program staff to do this important follow-up to create future opportunities.

Taking donors on a tour of a critical service your nonprofit provides its clients leaves a lasting positive impression on them. They see with their own eyes the difference their gift is making in the community. This is one example of how the Resource Development Department cultivates relationships with donors in order to increase their giving.

The bottom line is the investment required to establish a well-run Resource Development Department will pay for itself in the long run. By well-run, I mean you have a firm grasp of your nonprofit's revenue, which you'll use to set benchmarks and goals that the department must meet to justify its existence. In each nonprofit I led that didn't have a Resource Development Department, I worked to establish it as quickly as possible, but it usually took me about twelve months to receive approval and fill positions. Once the department was fully operating, the nonprofit saw its return on investment.

For you fortunate CEOs that have a Resource Development Department already in place, you must take a deep dive into how it is run and identify its strengths and fix its weaknesses. Refer to the checklist in chapter 5, "Framework 1: One-on-One Meetings during Your First Ninety Days," to assess your current Resource Development Department and what additional tools it needs to generate even greater results.

What's in Your Nonprofit's Portfolio?

WHEN YOU'RE JUST WEEKS AND MONTHS into your job, you may feel like you're speeding down the highway and changing a flat tire at the same time. Being responsible to raise money using the fundraising model you inherited and simultaneously addressing weaknesses and introducing your own powerful strategy are monumental tasks. To manage these two enormous responsibilities well, break them down into two parts:

First, dissect the pieces of your nonprofit's current fundraising portfolio's pie through the financial statements. In the annual operating budget, the audited annual income statement will show the revenue your organization generated in the prior year. The balance sheet and cash flow report give you the information necessary to assess your organization's fiscal health and in particular its revenue as outlined in the audited income statement from the prior year.

Second, identify the strategies that were part of putting together the operating budget you inherited in the current fiscal year. From there, ask your CFO for the current fiscal year's most recent unaudited income statement, which was generated when closing the nonprofit's books every month. With the unaudited income statement in your hands, you'll begin to understand how financial information is presented to the board monthly, as well as the assumptions made for budgeting expenses. For now, focus on the revenue line and how it was established. Ask yourself:

1. What are the detailed budget explanations of how many individual contributions and grants are planned for this year?
2. What is the total dollar amount for each line item contributing to the total annual budgeted revenue? (The same type of detailed information should be requested for all grants and events and every other revenue line for the current fiscal year's budget goal.)

XYZ Nonprofit's Unaudited Income Statement Review

IMAGINE YOU'VE JUST BEEN HIRED AS XYZ's CEO. You ask your Finance Department for the unaudited monthly income statement, which lists the operating revenue and expenses for the current fiscal budget year. The following is an example of this document:

XYZ Nonprofit
Income Statement – Unaudited
For Two Months Ended August 31, 20XX

	YTD Actual 7/1/20XX- 8/31/20XX	YTD Budget 7/1/20XX - 8/31/20XX	Annual Budget Fiscal Year 20XX
OPERATING REVENUE			
Contributions & Grants	$1,501,675	$1,454,577	$7,100,000
Events (net)	$389,065	$414,758	$2,500,000
Other Gifts	$45,907	$45,833	$300,000
Foundations & Trusts	$16,699	$38,333	$530,000
Endow. Draw	$728,088	$711,579	$500,000
Fees	$72,804	$66,733	$125,000
Total Op. Rev.	$2,754,238	$2,731,813	$11,055,000
OPERATING EXPENSES			
Program Svcs.	$1,290,867	$1,348,213	$6,500,277
Program Admin.	$89,992	$65,719	$390,000
Development	$47,340	$41,000	$248,000
Grant Programs	$760,145	$833,750	$2,202,536
Administration	$137,532	$148,750	$890,000
Fundraising	$128,584	$134,468	$800,000
Total Op. Exp.	$2,454,460	$2,571,900	$11,030,813
NET OPERATING INCOME	$299,778	$159,913	$24,187

Early in my tenure at all the nonprofits where I worked, I dug into the unaudited income statement for the month I came on board as CEO. With insights from my CFO and other senior management team members, this helped me understand what was in the annual operating budget for the current fiscal year.

Within nonprofits are different types of fundraising activities. Let's explore each revenue line where you'll learn questions you should ask to perform your analysis. As you follow along with this process, think about how you will ultimately do the same for the nonprofit you will be leading.

Contributions and Grants:
XYZ Annual Budget of $7.1 Million

HAVING A COMMON UNDERSTANDING of key concepts is central to effectively investigating the vast topic of the role that contributions and grants play in fundraising. To begin, what is the difference between contributions and grants? Contributions are gifts, usually from individuals or businesses, that typically have no restrictions or stipulations. Foundations and government entities give grants through an application process and follow specific rules for allocating the grant amount. Next, fundraising is obtaining voluntary financial contributions from individuals, businesses, charitable foundations, and government agencies. A nonprofit uses these contributions to grow and meet the needs of the community it serves.

Under this definition, contributions and grants are one part of XYZ's fundraising activities where it appeals to individual donors, businesses, charitable foundations, and government entities for support. The following are fundamental questions you need to ask the resource development leader, grant writer, and CFO to understand what this $7.1 million contributions and grants line consists of:

1. How many contributions and grants are in the $7.1M annual budget line item?
2. Who are the contributors? List them by name and whether they are individual donors, corporate givers, or both budgeted for this year.
3. What are the names of each entity providing the organization a grant?
4. Which of these grants are given by charitable foundations and which by government funders?
5. For government grants, what is the government agency providing the grant—federal, state, county, or municipal?
6. How much was budgeted in the annual operating budget for each grant?
7. How much in this budget line was estimated for new contributions and grants? From whom will these potential funds come?
8. Have we received contributions and grant money from these sources in the past? If so, what is their giving history of support?
9. Is the amount of the grant what was originally applied for or was it less?
10. Is it a multi-year grant or a grant with a specific ending date?
11. If not a multi-year grant, must or can it be reapplied for each year?

12. Who is the person the nonprofit deals with to receive the funds from the grantor?
13. Does the CFO have a finance contact if the grant has certain financial stipulations?
14. What staff person has the relationship in the organization for each contributor and grant maker?
15. What is the purpose of the funding?
16. Is the contribution or grant restricted to a certain program or unrestricted and can be used for general operating?
17. Does the contribution or grant provide reimbursement for a specific activity or program run by the nonprofit?
18. Has the organization met the full grant each year the grant was given? That is, did the organization meet the full amount of the grant by providing the services in the community?
19. What reporting requirements are there for any contribution or grant?
20. What other requirements must be met for future funding considerations?

While you'll be asking for an immense amount of information about each contribution and grant, the development leader or the grant writer or both who secured the funds in the past and built the budget this year with the CFO should be able to answer these questions quickly. These people are also responsible to maintain documentation and all the files for each individual contribution and grant. The CFO is another source to help answer these questions because he or she is documenting the financial activity for each contribution and grant in both the revenue and expense streams monthly.

Right away, the answers you receive show if the nonprofit has a strong development strategy.

Your analysis also includes determining if the development and finance systems run on the same software platform. If not, this can become a major obstacle in your efforts to grow and develop XYZ. The best way to build a solid resource development strategy is to make sure the software the Resource Development and Finance Departments use is compatible. This allows your team to maintain data the Resource Development, Program/Direct Service Delivery, and Finance Departments have verified and then agreed upon. Such vetted, high-quality data improves development strategies when processing gifts and maintaining vital donor information.

In my case, I was a vice president of resource development turned CEO. Upon beginning my role as leader of my nonprofit, I knew effective resource development software was essential for our department to meet our goals. If we didn't have it, I obtained it right away. The same need for software applies to each department in your nonprofit. With today's software capable of sophisticated analytics and generating fine-tuned data, your decisions are able to be data driven to an unprecedented degree. Making intelligent use of macro and micro data is how successful organizations, including nonprofits, stay competitive. Thus, obtaining the best software tools possible is a key to your nonprofit's high achievement.

For XYZ, the $7.1 million represents a whopping 64.2 percent of the $11 million of its annual operating revenue. Because contributions and grants typically provide a significant amount of funding for many nonprofits, you must have a thorough understanding of the contribution and grant process. In the case of XYZ, its contributions accounted for $2.1 million, and the grant breakdown is $1 million federal, $1.2 million state, $1.1 million county, $0.5 million municipal, and $1.2 million charitable foundations. Given the number of sources and the dollar amounts of each, this portfolio is well diversified, but you need to review the details of each grant and gift, as described in the preceding list of questions. If one funding source suddenly disappeared, the nonprofit would be financially bruised but would not collapse.

If, upon your investigation, you find out XYZ's funding came from only contributions and one grant source, you would take action right away. Delving deeper into its funding, you need to determine if the lack of diversification is fiscally wise (which is unlikely) or if you need to perform a portfolio overhaul (which is likely). In either case, your job is to assess the strengths and weaknesses of the portfolio, and like a financial advisor, you can do this only through thorough portfolio analysis.

In general, what is a solid revenue mix? For most nonprofits, the industry standard for the top-four funding sources are individual contributions, gifts from businesses, fees, and grants. XZY reflects this type of well-diversified portfolio.

Events (Net):
XYZ Annual Budget of $2.5 Million

EVENTS ARE SOCIAL GATHERINGS THE NONPROFIT hosts for the community to raise awareness of the organization, its mission, and often a specific need. Examples of events are fundraising runs and walks, gala dinners, and golf tournaments. As part of most of these events, the nonprofit may have live and silent auctions, speaking presentations about the mission, appeals for individual contributions, and entertainment for attendees.

The purposes of events are as follows:

- Attract new donors
- Solicit donations from past donors who attend the event annually
- Recognize existing donors, sponsors, and volunteers of the event
- Highlight the importance of the mission of the organization
- Provide opportunities to make in-person, meaningful connections, for example, through presentations and solicitations to hundreds of attendees who are donors or potential donors. Every event must have an *ask* component where representatives of the nonprofit connect in a meaningful way with attendees and then ask for a donation. By establishing a relationship with as many attendees as possible, the organization increases the likelihood that many will donate to it.
- Generate leads comprising potential donors and volunteers. With a Resource Development Department performing effective follow-up, these potential donors may turn into passionate and generous benefactors.

In XYZ, the events (net) line makes up $2.5 million, or 22.6 percent of the nonprofit's operating revenue. *Net* is important because that indicates the revenue generated minus the expenses paid for the event. The resulting net revenue is what helps fund XYZ's operation and mission.

As XYZ's CEO, you need to ask the following questions in order to learn about each event:

1. How many events is the organization planning to put on in this fiscal year that are budgeted in the $2.5M net figure?
2. What are the names and dates of each event to be conducted during the fiscal year?
3. Are there any multi-day events the organization will put on?
4. If so, what is the detailed budget for each day of the multi-day event? This information is needed because each day of a multi-day event will have revenues and costs related to it.
5. Also if so, what is the net revenue for each day of the multi-day event? This clearly points out what day is the most crucial, where the majority of funds are raised, and if any day is losing money.
6. What is the history of success for each event showing the net revenue numbers that were generated in prior years? Go back as far as possible to review the net numbers.
7. Is there a particular theme or group of people the event is geared to attract?
8. Are the founding members of the event still involved with the organization in putting the event together?
9. How is the event chair for each event selected each year?
10. How many people—both volunteers and staff—are involved for each event? Size does matter, especially for multi-day events. Don't just look at volunteers. Also consider what is required for staff to carry out a multi-day event.

11. Are board members active and engaged for each event to make it successful? Depending upon the format of the event, their commitments may include but are not limited to soliciting sponsors and selling tables and tickets.
12. Do board and committee members actively secure live and silent auction items?
13. What other contributions do committee members make for each event?
14. How do board and committee members assist in promoting/marketing the event within their network of contacts and within the community?
15. What is the budgeted net revenue for each event? (After the event takes place, compare the event's budgeted net revenue to the actual net revenue raised.)
16. What is each event's detailed budget that shows the revenue to be generated minus its expected expenses? The details should include:
    REVENUE
    a. Sponsorships
    b. Contributions of affinity groups associated with the event
    c. Live auction items
    d. Silent auction items
    e. Contributions and gifts from attendees
    f. Other revenue that may be generated from the event
    EXPENSES
    a. Rental of facilities
    b. Food and beverage
    c. Entertainment
    d. Other direct expenses

17. Did the volunteer committee members and staff for each event put the proposed event budget together? If so, was this part of the budgeting process when the budget was approved by the board for the current fiscal year? Or was the budget developed by staff and then reviewed with the board for approval?

For events to be successful, they must have planning that includes strict and well-thought-out budgeting. Planning addresses identifying the audience you want to attract. From there, you'll develop the strategies that align your work with your target attendees. In addition, you need to make the event personal. You do this by showing attendees the services and benefits it provides the community and why their support is meaningful and critical to meet the nonprofit's mission.

The measure of the efficacy of your planning and budgeting is an event's net proceeds. An industry standard for event return on investment (ROI) is at least 50 percent more than the cost for the event and staff time associated with it.

By asking the questions above, you'll understand what is in the current budget. In addition, the answers you receive will spark other questions regarding the event's ROI. One important question is:

> *How well did the organization meet its budgeted expenses for the event?*

On the one hand, if your revenue goals were met but you exceeded your budgeted expense goals, then your net return is less than it could have been. To make sure this doesn't happen again, you need to figure out why expenses exceeded the budgeted amounts. On the other hand, if you met both your revenue and expense goals (and maybe spent even less than you had budgeted), then your positive net return is a proud accomplishment. To repeat this feat, you need to figure out what went right and apply those effective practices to your future planning.

Other Gifts:
XYZ Annual Budget of $300,000

"OTHER GIFTS" IS A CATCH-ALL CATEGORY. It may include contributions received in memory of someone who has passed away. Or in a cause marketing campaign, a company may give a percentage of its profits on a particular day for your nonprofit. It may even be the dollars raised in a new online giving strategy you are testing.

As in the previous revenue categories, you must uncover the details of this line item. What are the historical factors for funds coming into the organization not part of your traditional fundraising activities but still an important part of your revenue stream?

In XYZ's budget, the $300,000 is 2.7 percent of its total revenue. While it may not seem like much, this amount still benefits the organization's net operating income. In your nonprofit, the same is true. Thus, always understand every line and detail of other gifts that come to your nonprofit that are reflected in this revenue line.

Do you have one-time donors who could be turned into annual givers because they are just waiting for your nonprofit to reach out to them? Does a partnership opportunity exist for potential program funding for your organization to continue as in the case of a cause marketing campaign?

As with each revenue item, does the budget for other gifts include estimates for new contributions and grants? And if so, from whom will these potential funds come?

Answering these questions well will create fundraising opportunities. This is another benefit of knowing your team. Understanding who within your nonprofit is responsible for putting together this budget line item allows you to uncover otherwise unidentified opportunities. Here is where your Resource Development Department will play an important role to boost contributions.

Foundations & Trusts: XYZ Annual Budget of $530,000

For XYZ, this line represents 4.8 percent of the operating revenue. Trusts are held and foundations are run by others, and XYZ is a beneficiary of these entities. From the foundation or the financial institution managing a trust, XYZ receives gifts on a quarterly or annual basis.

XYZ could become a trust or foundation's beneficiary through many ways. In addition, as you learned in Framework 1, volunteers and donors are a nonprofit's treasure hunters.

I once had a volunteer, Bric, who was a financial advisor. One of Bric's clients was an elderly woman who had no living relatives and a strong philanthropic disposition.

"To whom should I leave my estate after I pass?" Ellen asked Brian.

"Since I know how much you value giving, consider leaving your legacy to worthy charitable organizations that support your community and whose mission you believe in," Bric said.

With that advice, Ellen decided to gift her estate upon her passing to her church and our nonprofit. She respected how well both organizations were run and the important role we played in her community. She established a trust, and after her death, our nonprofit received her financial support.

I repeated Ellen's story to my board and staff to show how maintaining a strong connection with volunteers (Bric) and prospects (Ellen) can reap tremendous financial benefits.

As the new CEO, take the time to learn about the funds your nonprofit receives. By researching your nonprofit's history and knowing who will best answer your questions (for example, "How was the nonprofit named?"), you'll uncover countless opportunities to benefit your organization.

Endowment Draw:
XYZ Annual Budget of $500,000

IF YOUR ORGANIZATION IS FORTUNATE to have an endowment fund, then you are ahead of most nonprofits and will quickly see the benefit of having one. I believe that the establishment of an endowment fund for any nonprofit is a key factor in having a way to direct long-time donors to support your work after they are gone. It allows them to leave a legacy and to highlight it through a planned gift to your organization.

For XYZ, the endowment draw for this year is $500,000, which is 4.6 percent of its annual operating revenue. This amount is big enough that you must highlight this fund to your board as a major revenue benefit if it does not realize it already. The gifts that make up the endowment fund's principal provide the annual draw for your nonprofit. Therefore, identify the individuals and organizations that bestowed these gifts from which your nonprofit draws annually. This information provides your organization with the opportunity to celebrate those who left a financial legacy. It will also show your current contributors and your community that your organization continues to honor and thank those who support and improve the nonprofit, even after their passing.

I was fortunate to work with the Investment Committee of my nonprofit that managed these funds wisely. Through working closely with the committee and the organization we hired to invest our dollars according to our investment policy, I gained a solid understanding about how endowments work, including the importance of planned giving. I worked hard to convince others—our board and those donors who were passionate about our nonprofit—to consider writing our nonprofit into their wills and estate plans, along with any trusts they might have been establishing.

As a new CEO, take time to sit down with your CFO, as well as any staff that work on endowment gifts, to find out every person and organization that has made an endowment gift.

Use this information to find board volunteers who will champion the importance of planned giving. Volunteers are effective recruiting sources to make connections; instead of a cold appeal from your nonprofit to a potential donor, volunteers can sincerely reach out with warmth to those in their network. A simple, "Hey, come join me," that volunteers say to their family, friends, and colleagues can result in adding donors to your nonprofit's endowment society.

Their efforts may have generated estimates in the budget. Ask how much in the endowment draw's budget line was estimated for this year and from whom these potential funds will come.

At one nonprofit I led, I had a board member who committed a sizeable gift from her estate plan for our nonprofit. She not only provided her generous gift but also became our champion for planned giving. Benefitting from both her treasure and treasure-hunting skill was no accident.

In doing my homework, I discovered this board member was passionate in convincing others about the benefits of planned giving, so I asked her to join our nonprofit's planned-giving outreach programs. She became a highly effective advocate and created many important connections for us.

Similar to what I experienced, your efforts may provide massive dividends to your nonprofit. While you may not see the gifts immediately or even during your term as CEO, the work you do today with key volunteer leadership in establishing endowment funds and planned gift expectancies will benefit your nonprofit tomorrow. Your nonprofit's endowment supports its long-term viability, which is the lasting legacy you'll leave to your organization.

Fees: XYZ Annual Budget of $125,000

For XYZ, these fees make up 1.1 percent of its annual budget. As CEO, you must know to whom and for what the fees are being charged. For example, are they:

- for service or membership that the nonprofit requires for its clients to help cover costs?
- generated from providing training classes (such as parenting classes, first aid, and CPR) in the community related to the nonprofit's mission?

- related to other activities the organization charges for during the fiscal year?

No matter what they may be for, you must understand why they are being charged, who collects them, and who estimated the amount for this line item in the annual budget.

First, Know Your Revenue; Next, Know Your Expenses

"Boss, the AC has gone out. And I think this time around it's beyond repair," my staff member told me.

"From upgrading obsolete computers to replacing entire HVAC systems, this is the glamorous life of a CEO," I thought to myself.

While I wasn't happy to hear the bad news, I knew that having to figure out how to cover unexpected expenses that were not budgeted was one of the many diverse hats I wore.

So far, you've learned how to perform an initial analysis of your nonprofit's revenue. Now, you need to ask yourself, "What are the expenses telling me?"

Expenses sometimes not covered in the budget are capital, infrastructure, technology upgrades, new software for the nonprofit's programs, and equipment. Whether covered or not, you'll need to figure out how you'll raise money to pay for these often-big-ticket items.

As you review your nonprofit's unaudited income statement, you'll see expense items pop up as being in the red because they exceed their monthly budgeted estimates. This is where the monthly closing of the books is important. You'll use this information when you speak with your CFO and ask why expenses are exceeding the monthly estimates. I can say through experience that a solid CFO will never hold back regarding any bad financial news because of the required reporting you provide to the board each month. Some items aren't easily identified as being covered by your nonprofit's revenue, or only if you break the items out can you tell they are connected to multiple revenue categories in the unaudited income statement. When it comes to your investigation of costs, your job is to determine if they are all—both unexpected and planned expenses—covered by the revenue your nonprofit has raised. As you analyze your revenue, be on the lookout for missing items such as infrastructure.

As you see, the unaudited income statement for XYZ has no indication of capital or equipment needs within the current document. Because of the organization's size, those items are likely addressed somewhere in the budget, but you should always check to be certain. I recommend creating such lines in the unaudited monthly financial statement so the board knows the financial needs within the nonprofit and can foresee when expenses may occur.

I worked with my finance chair and CFO to revise the monthly income statement to break items out that were otherwise difficult to identify. In addition, I always notified the Executive Committee and board, explaining why I had the Finance Department separate out these items in the statement.

By infrastructure, I'm referring not just to the nonprofit's building. It can include filling parking lot potholes that could lead to injury and lawsuits if left in disrepair. There are also sidewalks, fencing, security cameras inside and out, HVAC systems, roofs, and a mountain of other items that are part of infrastructure.

Once you determine your expenses, you're ready to work with your Resource Development Department to create plans to raise the revenue necessary to cover your nonprofit's costs. Or in my case, I did not have such a department at the time so I was charged to figure this out with the people on my team who were working to generate revenue when I walked through the door as the new CEO. As you learned in Framework 1, ask to see the rolling five-year capital budget plan that highlights the work to be done each year. If your organization does not have this, I highly recommend you implement one.

In every nonprofit I led that didn't have a Resource Development Department, stress and uncertainty spread throughout the nonprofit like a bad cold when we were struck by huge and unexpected expenses that are inevitable within any year, given the organization's large and complex operations. Without a Resource Development Department, a well-coordinated development strategy didn't exist. As a consequence, the nonprofit ran the risk of being in the red due to insufficient funds to cover unexpected expenses in the budget. It was then my responsibility as CEO to develop a recommendation to address such items.

As you read previously, I always made it a priority to establish a Resource Development Department as quickly as possible. I also made sure our nonprofit had a plan in place to tackle big future expenses after I identified them and tasked this responsibility to the Resource Development Department under my direction. This was yet another reason why establishing this department was a top priority.

In the case of my nonprofit's air conditioning system that needed to be replaced, we didn't have a budget item to cover that. Thus, we put the expense under the repair and maintenance category. I then prepared an explanation to the board with my CFO and finance chair to report the high repair and maintenance cost when they reviewed the budget. In fact, we hoped someone would ask us in-depth questions because I looked forward to describing the necessary upgrades we were making. Inevitably, one fastidious board member asked, "Brian, I get why we are spending so much money in the repair and maintenance line, but how will you make sure we're not caught off-guard with such a huge expense in the future?" From there, I explained that replacing the air conditioning system, while costly, in the long run was cheaper than continually repairing a tired, old system.

Meanwhile, other facilities in this line item also needed equipment repairs and replacement. Without a budget to cover such expenses, I expected more conversations like this in the coming years. To facilitate future discussions—and ultimately negate the need for them because the expenses would be anticipated—I described my plan for a five-year capital budget and equipment needs that would bring in new technology and software to replace the old. I was analyzing current data and would be making recommendations, which included establishing a development strategy and department and addressing other important items not covered under the current revenue-generation structure. By maintaining clear communication, I stopped any confusion and doubt about what I believed we needed to do in this area.

This is the last category of revenue on XYZ's income statement. Now we'll examine in more detail some of these sources of revenue.

Reviewing Annual Gifts

THE LAST MAJOR CATEGORY TO EVALUATE is annual gifts and how your nonprofit receives them. As CEO you're responsible to review annual gifts of individual donors and the giving societies your nonprofit has established that recognize and celebrate these supporters.

In following the advice of Framework 1, you have already acknowledged the top-ten donors. Now you must determine how many individual gifts your nonprofit receives annually through the giving societies it established. Within each category, look at the total number of donors, amount given, and average gift size. Ultimately, you need to calculate the total amount all individual donors have contributed and what the average total gift is for the organization. Also, if your nonprofit is a part of a national federation, you'll likely have access to information about organizations so you can compare how your individual-donor giving compares to other entities of your size. Such benchmarking you'll probably perform for not just individual donors but also for overall development activities of similarly sized organizations.

After you have collected this information, you're now ready to think about how you will use it and whom you'll share it with it.

An Abundance Mindset: Setting Your Resource Development Strategy and Department

MY CEO TIME MANAGEMENT RULE OF THUMB is that about 50 percent of your total time should be spent with your board and staff in developing resources—planning, strategizing, and raising money for the organization.

When it comes to your resource development strategy, always come from a mindset of abundance. This means you seek opportunity everywhere and seize it with razor-sharp focus and commitment. On the other hand, with a scarcity mindset, opportunity is limited; thus your potential to grow is restricted as well. A scarcity mindset can turn into a crutch where you come up with countless excuses why your nonprofit is underperforming. Whether it's the stingy donor base in your community, the poor economy, or weaknesses within your team, a CEO can think of any number of reasons to explain why the nonprofit is limited in its fundraising capacity. While some reasons may be legitimate, an abundance mindset is much more effective than a scarcity one, even under an adverse fundraising landscape.

For proof, look at the best funded agencies in your community. Is their high achievement a result of pure luck?

Explore deeply, and you'll most likely discover they are hustling and developing relationships with anyone that has the potential to promote their mission. Their board members, volunteer donors, and staff are working tirelessly on behalf of the cause. If your current organization doesn't reflect an abundance mindset, then it's time to change its culture.

My approach as a new CEO was to analyze the unaudited financial statement revenue lines, especially those dealing with individual gifts. Afterward, I shared this information with my board chair and vice chair. I then requested them to consider arranging a meeting with the executive committee leadership with a single-item agenda: to review my findings of the unaudited financial revenue lines. During that meeting, I described the next steps I had in mind, which included establishing a Resource Development Department. With the support of my executive board leadership and direct reports, I usually presented my proposal to board members during an organizational development retreat with the goal of seeking approval to establish the department.

I took this direction because one of the main reasons I was hired as CEO was my pledge to raise more money for the nonprofit. In your case, this was likely one of the grounds for your hire too. Thus if a board is expecting you to raise money, you must devise a game plan, which is your resource development strategy.

Although my strategy differed in my three CEO assignments, one common thread was I always worked with my board leadership and Executive Committee to share my next key steps. In two nonprofits, I established a Resource Development Department, and in the third, the department already existed.

In addition, all three nonprofits were affiliated with a national organization or federation. For CEOs like me, these affiliations offered tools such as a national resource development staff and a national office liaison assigned to me.

These benefits provided powerful sources for recommendations and networking. I asked these staff members how other organizations of my nonprofit's size structured their Resource Development Departments and for the contact information of nonprofits with larger budgets. I then reached out directly to these organizations to see if they had practices worth emulating—why bother going through trial and error when you could instantly adopt a well-established efficient and effective process? These liaisons also helped me coordinate a retreat for the board or development strategy or both, and they participated in it as our national representative. They also provided contacts for consultants who were working with others in the federation on similar issues like development.

The support of professionals outside our nonprofit, such as liaisons, illustrated the extent to which people wanted our organization to thrive. In the end, our success also reflected well upon them. The input they provided helped me make a compelling case to my board to establish and staff a Resource Development Department, which ultimately created a development strategy. With the success of other nonprofits' development departments to use as examples, I was able to demonstrate the importance of our nonprofit to have one too.

Even though I always had a vision on how I wanted to structure my Resource Development Department, the national office's resources prepared me with counterarguments to address any potential objections from my board to setting up the department.

For those of you not part of a national organization or federation, look to local foundations and donors who currently give to your nonprofit and seek their advice on how to strengthen your development work. Also, don't be shy to connect with other successful agencies in your community and to take steps similar to the ones I did with my national organization. Remember that people generally are eager to help. I certainly was always more than willing to assist other agencies in my community in improving their resource development efforts. This included providing them with information on consultants I knew of through my local and national networks. By following my recommendation to reach out, my

CEO colleagues outside national organizations or federations have improved their development skills.

I also approached my local community funders and individual donors to express my desire for creating a more robust development strategy. This was one way I addressed **donor fatigue**, which is a type of burnout where people stop contributing to a nonprofit they once did give to. There are many reasons for this, including feeling a nonprofit is too often asking for their Three Ts. They may also feel the organization is putting little effort into growing its donor base. In other words, their perception leads them to think they're the only ones being asked to give, and thus they become reluctant to do so. They ask themselves, "Is the nonprofit reaching out to others just as much as it's appealing to me?" By describing my ambitious outreach work, I let current donors know that I rejected complacency, appreciated their generosity immensely, and would never take them for granted by relying solely on their support.

In one of my experiences, the national team I was working with said it had resources via a national grant for development purposes. The national team offered a matching grant for the local nonprofit I was leading. Given this lucrative opportunity, I started pitching it to board members, their companies, local foundations, and individual donors I believed would be interested. By announcing this grant, I was also countering donor fatigue.

We found local donors to provide the match for the initial grant. By maintaining an abundance mindset, I knew that even those who rejected my solicitation developed or maintained a positive view of our nonprofit. They knew that as its new CEO, I was working hard to obtain grants intended to improve our nonprofit. In fact, one donor who declined my appeal invited me to follow up with the outcome of the development study that the grant funded.

"If the results are compelling, then I may be interested in providing my support for the recommendations in it."

I did as he requested and met with him to provide the results of the study the grant paid for. It recommended creating a development position to support the strategies that would address critical needs not currently being funded. The donor agreed to fund it not just for one year but for several. I was able to benefit from this opportunity only by steadfastly upholding an abundance mindset. Rather than accept his initial rejection as a definitive no, I realized he was giving me an opening to work harder to uncover other avenues to gain his support. With an abundance mindset, you too will realize opportunities that would have otherwise remained hidden.

Part IV

Bringing It All Together

Chapter 12

Framework 5: The *Who*

> **In this chapter, you'll learn:**
>
> - the most important question to ask yourself every day;
> - that the *who* matters more than the *what*, but both must be considered;
> - to always have a quantifiable measurement of success for your programs and services;
> - specific methods to prepare volunteers to be powerful fundraisers.

IN ONE NONPROFIT I LED, children who exited our doors to return home most likely were going to bed hungry at night because of the lack of food in their houses. This meant, for these kids, the next nutritious meal was most likely at school the following day, when they received their free or reduced lunch. How can children be expected to pay attention in their classrooms, let alone learn difficult concepts, when their stomachs are churning out of hunger because their refrigerators and kitchen cabinets are empty?

Within another nonprofit, our headquarters were temporarily located on a military training center totally removed from the community. In fact, it was behind a security fence with a checkpoint operated by military police. How could the community receive the critical resources and services it needed if the nonprofit didn't have an easily accessible, permanent home?

These are just two examples among many of needs and problems I identified within nonprofits and their communities during my self-onboarding process. The hallmark of high-performance CEOs is an ability not just to address *any* problem but also to solve extraordinarily big, complicated ones that will most benefit the communities the nonprofit serves. In fact, the best CEOs have a near obsession of wanting to take on problems of four-alarm-fire magnitude and ambitious, large-scale projects where other less willing and less able leaders would run in the opposite direction as fast as possible.

In fact, we nonprofit CEOs are a rare and courageous breed of leader! We're willing to take massive, calculated risk and put our reputations on the line if it means doing so will help as many people as possible. We're fueled by compassion and our nonprofit's mission and guided by our wisdom, expertise, discipline . . . and gut.

Upon discovering obstacles, I strived to bring about enduring, status-quo-breaking, positive change during my tenure as CEO. This often required playing the role of a talented and principled politician who needs to please many different constituencies in order to push through his agenda. The nonprofit depended on my leadership, and I sought to leave the organization better than how I found it. This was part of the legacy as a compassionate leader that I handed to the next CEO.

As CEO, if you cannot express specific and clear examples of your nonprofit's impact in plain English that nearly anyone in your community understands, then you're not doing your job effectively. In the end, your legacy is not about buying an expensive and sophisticated software package whose advanced features you can speak at length about or the stunning new building that makes a bold statement to everyone who sees it. Rather, your duty is to show how these resources improve the lives of those your nonprofit serves—community members who are the most vulnerable and in need of help.

Along with the tremendous responsibility of being a peak-performing CEO comes the need to be enormously creative. When you unleash your creativity within the rules of engagement and constraints of the Frameworks you've read so far, you also unleash the full potential of your nonprofit's ability to serve its community, solve huge problems, and address major needs that would otherwise go unmet.

The previous four Frameworks have provided a roadmap of your journey ahead. From day one, you're setting the tone and vision for the future of your organization. You are planning, strategizing, and directing others in the day-to-day operations of your nonprofit. Beyond the everyday work, you're identifying where the greatest needs are. You're also determining areas where you can grow critical services your nonprofit provides or developing more and stronger partnerships to expand upon the work you already do. You may do this through observing how information is gathered if the data-collecting tools you use are outdated. Or you may extend opportunities to uncover and develop additional relationships with potential donors. You may also create an outreach strategy that generates relationships and fosters new revenue opportunities.

In this chapter, we'll bring it all together. The four previous Frameworks poured the foundation for your leadership path. In this final Framework, you'll learn key concepts that, when combined with what you've read so far, will help you tap into your greatest leadership potential and provide a roadmap to CEO excellence.

The Most Important Question to Ask Yourself Every Day

EACH MORNING AS A CEO, I parked my car in the lot and did a short reflection. I asked myself, "Why did you decide to become a CEO?"

I always had the same answer, "To help the community members I'm responsible to serve."

After leaving my car and entering the office, I had a range of responsibilities—from ones that needed my attention right away to others that could wait—staring at me on my computer screen. Some I knew ahead of time, such as planning a major fundraising event, while others I didn't, such as when a newbie driver mistook the brake for the gas pedal and crashed into one of our service center locations (fortunately, no one was injured).

Regardless of how many big problems I had to solve that day, all the solutions had one larger objective: improving the lives of community members. And my question at the start of the day reminded me of that. Every action I took as the hours passed in the workday needed to positively affect those we were charged to serve.

Some days I was completely exhausted after addressing a nonstop series of headaches. Other days I was on a euphoric high after meeting a major milestone or a series of them with aplomb. Regardless of the ups and downs that are part of the leadership rollercoaster ride, constantly reminding myself why I became a CEO brought immense purpose and meaning to my work. Whether my day was disappointing or delightful, by always focusing on my purpose, I was able to maintain the motivation and passion necessary to persevere past obstacles and meet my nonprofit's most ambitious objectives.

Focus on the *Who* More than the *What*

WHEN IT COMES TO *what work to do* versus *who will benefit from it,* CEOs must focus on creating a balance between the two. All too often, I've witnessed otherwise talented CEOs inadvertently fall into the trap of overly concentrating on the *what*, and as a consequence, they neglect to pay attention to the *who*. But the *who* should always come first because that's what the nonprofit exists to serve—the community and its members.

Both *who* and *what* are necessary and important. But too much *what* emphasis results in meeting short-term needs at the expense of solving deeper problems through long-term solutions. Put another way, *what* addresses immediate issues, and *who* goes far beyond that to solving long-term problems:

- Sometimes the *what* and the *who* work well together.
- Other times addressing too much *what* results in neglecting the *who*.

We'll explore each in the following two case studies.

When the *What* and the *Who* Work Well Together

IN THE CASE OF THE CHILDREN who were going to bed hungry, the short-term and urgent problem we had to address was *what* we needed to do first. Creating the snack program attended to this immediate need upon their arrival to our nonprofit, and we were proud of what a big, positive impact it made in our members' lives.

I always identified with those I was helping. While never impoverished growing up, by no means was I raised in a well-off family. My parents both worked, and in my dad's case, he held down two jobs. The time my mom and dad spent away from home to maintain what we had in our lives meant my three siblings and I were latchkey kids before the term became commonplace. While we didn't receive services like the ones the nonprofits provided that I later led, plenty of families in my community did, which speaks to the socioeconomics of where I grew up.

As the youngest in a loving family with parents who worked tirelessly to support us and growing up in a community where I saw poverty, I was drawn to the vocation of being a servant leader for those in need. Using my past as a guide, I always reminded myself of why I woke up each day to devote all my professional hours to meeting my nonprofit's mission.

All of us have a background and story that led us to our current career as a nonprofit CEO. What's yours? Reflecting on your answer will bring about great clarity to be an excellent leader now and into the future.

In the case of the snack program within my nonprofit, thinking deeply about *who* needed to be fed exposed deeper issues within the lives of the youths we served over the long term: living in food deserts with no big-box grocery stores in their neighborhoods, food insecurity in the home, and their performance within our various academic intervention programs and, more importantly, at their schools. (As a testament to the foresight and commitment of past board and staff leadership, the nonprofit was established in the community in 1965 to meet the critical needs of children living in these underserved areas.) We concluded that, in addition to the snack they received after walking through our doors after school, they also needed a meal before they left our facilities and returned home at night. Furthermore, we wanted the program to continue when school was not in session. Summer vacation was no break for us or our kids. They participated in our Summer Food Program and thus received needed nourishment all year long.

I implemented the program by lobbying the board of directors to back it and then applying and qualifying for funding from the Afterschool Meals Program (AMP), which offers a free healthy snack and hot meal Monday through Friday and Saturdays during the school year. AMP is part of the federal government's Child Care Food Program and funded through the US Department of Agriculture, Food and Nutrition Service and administered through the state's Department of Health. It provided nutritious foods children might not receive due to limited income or insufficient information at home on healthy eating. All snacks and meals met nutritional requirements set by the state, and we provided parents a monthly menu at the beginning of each program year.

For us to qualify for funding for Saturday snacks and meals, federal and state mandates required nonprofits to provide the same Monday-through-Friday enrichment programs to the youth on Saturdays. Therefore, for the forty-two Saturdays we provided meals, we had our math and reading programs, healthy lifestyle classes, homework tutoring, and physical education activities. To cover costs for these Saturday programs, I found a foundation that generously paid for staff, activities, utilities, and cleanup.

As for most government programs, qualifying and then maintaining compliance was an enormous task. To complicate matters further, we were the first nonprofit in the state to apply for this new program, so we couldn't receive recommendations and advice from nonprofits that had previously qualified for it. In the end, completing the onerous application, staying on top of the mountain of paperwork afterward, and meeting filing deadlines were worth the effort.

For Every Program and Service Your Nonprofit Provides, Always Have a Measurement of Success

WITH TODAY'S SOPHISTICATED SOFTWARE and your skill at assessing your team and organization following what you've learned in this book, you have an abundant source of detailed information to track and measure your nonprofit's performance.

From your departments and staff to your volunteers, you're able to evaluate your nonprofit on a daily, weekly, and monthly basis. You're continually ensuring you have the right people in the right leadership positions and quickly making the necessary staffing changes in order to build the team you'll need to accomplish your big objectives. This level of constant appraisal is how you maintain high achievement and demonstrate to your board with razor-sharp precision the nonprofit's performance under your leadership. When you're doing remarkable work, such as spearheading an ambitious program, turning around a struggling department or entire nonprofit, or building upon the strong organization you inherited, you both embrace and insist on a high standard of transparency. Your bold "bring it on!" attitude reveals your willingness to let your outcomes demonstrate your leadership prowess.

As you complete the tasks and recommendations in each Framework, you always want to make sure you're on the right track and constantly adapting to change, both of which are essential to high achievement. The data you have compiled will inform your decisions and the innovations that you'll implement to fulfill your pledges that convinced the hiring committee to appoint you.

Effectively holding yourself accountable is one of the hallmarks of high-performance leadership. This requires you to identify your strengths and weaknesses through the lens of unabashed objectivity. Throughout history, we've had countless examples of once brilliant leaders that fell from grace because they neglected to address their weaknesses, outright denied their faults, ignored the consequences of their poor judgment, or dismissed their poor decisions. CEOs avoid falling into this leadership trap by constantly evaluating their performance through unbiased and detailed metrics. One simple way to hold yourself accountable is to continually ask yourself, "What value are any of my given initiatives adding to my organization's mission?"

Since the start of the snack and meal program in our nonprofit, we had multiple means to measure its success. We provided over seven million snacks and meals to youth over the eleven years I served the nonprofit. The neighboring K through 12 public schools valued our role in the community and referred our program to their low-income youth in need of a safe, stable environment where they would be fed, given academic support, and provided supervision. After our successful inaugural year, the Florida Partnership to End Childhood Hunger recognized our nonprofit with the Trail Blazer Award for being the first afterschool entity to implement the program in the Sunshine State. Later, our national organization saw the success of our food program and promoted it to clubs nationwide. We became a resource for other nonprofits to implement the program in their communities through guidance and mentorship.

For our accomplishments, in May 2016, we received a national award for program excellence in the Health & Life Skills category at our 110th National Conference. This was a proud moment for all of us who worked so hard to serve our community's *who*—young people needing nutrition.

Serving meals to children who would otherwise go to bed hungry would not have happened if I hadn't moved beyond the *what* and dug deeply, determining the needs of our *who*. Imagine the powerful initiatives your nonprofit will come up with when you inspire and encourage your staff to remain steadfastly focused on your organization's *who*.

When Too Much *What* Results in Neglecting the *Who*

IN THE CASE OF THE NONPROFIT on a military training center the odd and remote location made sense from a *what to do* perspective. How could a nonprofit pass up the opportunity for a rent-free headquarters? That was the arrangement the organization's management and board leadership secured before I started my tenure. The nonprofit's leadership knew this great deal had an expiration date because the training center would close in four years. During the interview process, I found this out.

When I asked the logical follow-up question, "What's the plan for the new location?" I was told, "We don't have one."

This was far from reassuring. Actually, they did have a plan of sorts—for the new CEO to work with the board to take on this enormous responsibility. So from the start, I knew that if I was hired, I'd be charged to solve the nonprofit's biggest problem.

After learning more about the history behind the strange location, I concluded that the nonprofit agreed to the short-term lease for the donated space to buy itself time until it could come up with a long-term solution. The downside of this decision was that it led to procrastination. With a few years remaining in the contract, finding a permanent home lost its urgency. On a daily basis, so many pressing issues and emergencies spring up within any big organization. Thus it was easy to neglect addressing a problem that didn't need to be solved right away and thinking about the enormous task ahead ... let alone carrying out an exhaustively developed plan.

While the military base location made sense from a short-term fiscal perspective, it delayed addressing the *who will benefit from it*. Having this temporary home had several long-term drawbacks: Being behind the confines of a secure military training center on the main base made the nonprofit inaccessible to its most important constituent, the local community. In addition, because our organization had not done proper planning to find itself a permanent home, it limited our potential. We weren't able to serve our community, which included fundraising, to the best of our ability. Next, the allure of free rent was a huge crutch. It kept the nonprofit from focusing on where, in only four years, it would call home, which ideally would have been a permanent, prominent, and readily accessible place within the community. Just as children benefit from a stable home, so do nonprofits! All these downsides weakened the nonprofit's ability to better serve the *who* that most needed it.

When I became CEO, I performed the work described in Framework 1 during my self-onboarding. My investigation uncovered that the uninviting and secluded location resulted in people not bothering to go past the main gate, let alone enter our facility and take advantage of our resources.

My remedy was one that others before me did not want to tackle or even touch: executing a capital campaign for a new headquarters. In fact, even within the board when I asked members, "Hey folks, who would be a good choice to chair the capital campaign?" the response was unanimous.

"There's no way we'll do that because it will conflict with the Annual Campaign drive, including all the work the annual fund chair is doing with you and the resource development staff."

I identified a scarcity mindset within the nonprofit. According to my diagnosis, it was trapped in a cycle of excuses for not doing what I viewed as the most important step—focusing on the *who*. Solving this problem became my commitment, and I pledged to myself that I would break the nonprofit out of its culture of mediocrity. I certainly had not been hired to head an ordinary organization! We would have an abundance mindset from here forward, and I determined that the capital campaign would be the catalyst for it.

Being a CEO Is Demanding and Exciting

YOU'VE BEEN DESIGNATED THE ONE PERSON in the organization to identify and solve the biggest problems within your nonprofit. This points to the challenges and demands of taking on the CEO role. Not everyone has the ability or is cut out to be one. You always are looked upon to find answers to complex problems or to address difficult situations that existed long before you came onboard. You are often one of the last to be acknowledged for a job well done and the first to receive criticism when a problem arises.

After the tragedy of September 11, 2001, the broader economy tanked, and our nonprofit's revenues dwindled. In order to balance the budget and keep us strong until the economy improved, I needed to lay off ten people and implement a hiring freeze. During my discussions in our conference room with every individual being let go, some people cried—making me feel like the Grim Reaper, some sat silently and stoically in disbelief, and others understood why downsizing was necessary. There's no joy in holding these tough meetings but also no avoiding such unpleasant tasks. As CEO, you will inevitably need to implement reductions in force, and it humbles you. In the end, I knew my job was to keep the programs and services running and the remaining employees thriving, all to serve the community that needed us during this crisis and economic downturn.

As CEO, you're an exceptional breed of professional, and those who are like you are just as busy as you, taking on huge challenges. Thus as individuals consumed with meeting the endless needs of their organizations, CEOs are challenged to find peers and confidants. But when you do connect and then receive support from like-minded professionals, you'll benefit immensely from the camaraderie, their insight, and knowing they understand and appreciate the responsibility you carry within your organization.

I always enjoyed participating in CEO groups where I could share and gain thoughts and ideas. The men and women I've met have become trusted advisors and lifelong friends. Receiving mentorship and then being a guide to beginning CEOs are the most powerful experiences in my career. In fact, I was driven to write this book to help new CEOs because I know leadership is demanding, especially when you are starting out.

At the same time, heading a nonprofit is an exciting vocation. It's one where you'll meet people and have experiences that you otherwise would never have had and improve and save countless lives of those who would have no other means of support without your nonprofit.

Throughout my career, I've met and often worked closely with governors, mayors, county executives, business leaders, school board members, state and federal senators, celebrities, and entrepreneurs admired across the world. Why? Because these individuals have an interest in the work the nonprofit is performing in the community and want to improve the services and programs within it.

As far as my mission to change my nonprofit's culture from one of scarcity to abundance, I was on my own within my organization. But I had plenty of external support both inspiring and guiding me on how to do so. While the required effort can be demanding, I was also bolstered by the excitement I felt about doing what was right and necessary to serve the community.

From Scarcity to Abundance

WORKING WITHIN MY NONPROFIT'S CURRENT CULTURE of scarcity, I was on a one-man mission to bring about a culture of abundance. In addition, if I were to move forward with the capital campaign, I knew I would have to forego the standard strategy of electing a capital campaign chair and creating a committee that works with the CEO. If the nonprofit was to have a new building, I was going to lead the charge and enlist the help of a small but committed group of leaders who knew the challenge and were willing to face it. At the same time, under the careful watch of the annual campaign chair and committee, I had to make sure our major fundraising program met its objectives. They would not compete with each other. Rather, they both needed to be smash successes!

Thus we broke with conventional wisdom and created an unofficial capital campaign committee. I was its informal campaign chair, and past leadership committee volunteers were my kitchen cabinet. Thankfully, with the pending training center closure looming over us, the board backed the initiative under one very important condition—that no funds raised in the annual campaign would be used for the acquisition and renovation of the new building. I agreed and pledged to uphold that promise.

In order to keep our word and raise a ton of money, our small but powerful committee searched for new donors. We uncovered several that led to our ultimate success. At the same time, we also approached current corporate supporters to consider being a part of the capital campaign. We described how we would recognize them separately for their support of this special effort. If any donors were interested in giving to our capital campaign and were already supporting our annual campaign, I always requested that their donation not take away from their annual campaign contribution.

The more I made my compelling case for a new headquarters, the bigger and stronger my team became. By willing the capital campaign into existence, I brought on hard-working people willing to play a role in the campaign's success.

Preparing Volunteers to Be Powerful Fundraisers

HAVING A BOARD FILLED WITH VOLUNTEERS representing a diverse range of influential companies in your community is one of the hallmarks of your board-member recruiting success. Given the talent, professional skill, and powerful networks within each volunteer, you have remarkable potential to tap into and unleash.

I went to work right away setting my volunteers up for success using the same approach I followed in every fundraising effort throughout my career. My plan comprised the following:

1. Instill in volunteers the *people give to people* and abundance mindsets.
2. Perform thorough investigations and research on how donors have supported the organization and other agencies in various fundraising campaigns.
3. Connect the dots: provide volunteers the guidance to tap into their vast networks to benefit all fundraising campaigns.

4. Train and brief volunteers and rehearse with them before every call they make on behalf of the nonprofit.

1. Instill in Volunteers the *People Give to People* and *Abundance* Mindsets

YOUR VOLUNTEERS ARE LEADERS within their organizations and industries. They are C-levels, high-level managers, and entrepreneurs. What most of these men and women don't realize is that their role in your nonprofit positions them to extend their spheres of influence to become respected and well-known community leaders.

During our capital campaign when our volunteers and I made face-to-face calls to prospective donors, the executives on the other side of the table would often say to my volunteers, "You've got a demanding day job just like me. How do you possibly find the time to make calls for this nonprofit?"

Knowing that this point often came up during previous campaign calls, I used my experience as a professional fundraiser to prepare my volunteers for how they might respond. I encouraged them to describe how their belief in our mission motivated them to donate their time, talent, and treasure ... so their commitment compelled them to find time, despite their busy schedules. This impassioned and sincere explanation provided a great segue for the volunteer to introduce me to our prospective donors if we had never met before. If, however, we knew one another already, this became a great transition to discuss our appeal for them to consider. Thanking them for their time, the volunteer and I then described the purpose of our meeting.

Afterward, my volunteers and I debriefed. We went over what went well, what didn't, and the future steps we needed to take, such as sending thank-you cards or providing the prospects additional information for our promised follow-up from the meeting. If they couldn't contribute because of their pledge to our annual campaign, I always expressed heartfelt gratitude for their generosity. My volunteers and I noted the roles each of us played during the call and what we learned about the prospect and his or her company and placed our observations in our customer relationship management (CRM) software. We critiqued our performance by asking, "How effective was our strategy to call on people face-to-face in communicating the needs of the capital campaign?" Through our answers, we continually improved our prospecting calls on donors in the campaign.

As Linton Allen, founder of SunTrust Bank said, "If you build your community, you build your bank." No doubt Mr. Allen believed doing such things for the community would ultimately enhance his bank's profile and bottom line. Replace *bank* with *nonprofit*, and this statement perfectly describes when nonprofits build their communities, their fundraising initiatives benefit as well.

Inspire your volunteers to honor the nonprofit's past. Remind them to reflect on their predecessors who built the organization. Thanks to the tireless commitment of previous volunteers just like them, the nonprofit stands where it is today. Connect your current campaign with this legacy. Your volunteers are adding an important chapter in the storied history of your nonprofit.

Before every call, instill in your volunteers the concept of *people give to people* and the abundance mindset. Combined, they are powerful forces for all successful fundraising campaigns.

2. Perform Thorough Investigations and Research

As part of fulfilling Framework 1, I had face-to-face meetings with foundations, corporations, and individual donors that supported our nonprofit. I asked them about their history with our organization and what our nonprofit could do better to enhance our work together.

In addition, when I met with agency executives at their headquarters, I always had my detective hat on. I looked for sources of information such as donor walls or dedication plaques listing the names of individuals and companies that had contributed to their organization. These visits provided me with fantastic lists of people that could support the capital campaign. Together with my executive assistant and management team, we conducted research and collected names of potential donors that I would later consider contacting in my fundraising efforts with volunteers.

When I met with agency executives, I asked about their capital campaigns. They often told me useful information that I would note in my prospecting efforts.

From there, I'd inevitably receive a fascinating historical account. During these conversations, I often learned how donors had put the agency executives through a rigorous vetting process before finally agreeing to give. These tips helped me prepare for my calls and the briefing notes I provided my volunteers about prospective donors. The important details I compiled went beyond a list of names and could include the personalities and profiles of donors. This was essential intel I'd use when developing my donor prospect list.

3. Connect the Dots

PART OF INSTILLING AN ABUNDANCE MINDSET in your volunteers when it comes to fundraising is to provide them guidance. Although they are powerful executives representing large financial institutions, public accounting firms, entertainment companies, and more, they are often unaware of how their vast networks can contribute to a successful campaign. Your job is to connect the dots for them so they know they are the right person at the right time to call the business leader on behalf of your nonprofit.

Thus I asked volunteers questions about the businesses we would call on and any intel they might have through their networks. Did they have further insight or, better yet, any direct connections with these individuals or businesses that would benefit our capital campaign?

I used all this information to open doors, prepare my volunteers to speak on behalf of our nonprofit, and develop the most refined appeal possible to our prospective donors.

4. Train and Brief Volunteers and Rehearse with Them

STEPS 1 THROUGH 3 are your analysis and homework stages. Now you must prepare your plans to make your appeal. If your prospecting campaign is a meal, then you've set an impeccable table. It's time to invite your guests to a banquet they can't resist.

While you may think your volunteers would be reluctant to contact prospective donors on behalf of your nonprofit, you'd be surprised. After showing my volunteers how they would be the best person to make the appeal, sometimes other volunteers argued that they, in fact, were better qualified. In other words, volunteers would state their case like an experienced litigator in court, explaining why they would be the best person to make the call! That is a measurement of success for the three previous steps.

In addition, I did receive unsolicited support from some current and past board leadership. They recognized the urgency to solve the problem because they had been a part of the decision to move the nonprofit into the military training center. As a result of their board tenure with us, they were ideal candidates to make capital campaign appeals with me. In particular, they were well-suited to explain to potential donors why the prestigious and prominent businesses they represented on our board were supporting our nonprofit and the capital campaign. Having well-known companies pledging to our campaign served as a magnet motivating others to join. Thus I convinced them to fundraise on our nonprofit's behalf by contacting individuals in their powerful networks. When applicable, they used the quid-pro-quo fundraising strategy that says, "I helped you in your campaign. Can you help me in mine?"

These volunteers were our nonprofit's treasure hunters for our capital campaign. As business leaders themselves, they had colleagues and peers who were also captains of industry. Some of these business leaders that my treasure hunters would call on had either led or were a part of a capital campaign committee for another nonprofit in the community.

To make our initial call as effective as possible, I was responsible to train and brief volunteers and rehearse with them. This included preparing scripts, practicing the flow of the meeting, and addressing inevitable objections with solid counterarguments. For those volunteers who were happy to make the call but reluctant to ask for support, I always reassured them that I would fulfill that role.

If the volunteer was willing to be the opener, I was more than delighted to be the closer. Think of this as a dance. We will perform well only if our moves are impeccably choreographed and rehearsed and we know our roles perfectly.

These four steps are your action plan to turning prospects into donors who generously give to your nonprofit. I can guarantee nobody will be better prepared by following these steps. I have had a 100 percent success rate in every nonprofit campaign I've participated in because I've organized, planned, and practiced better than most other CEOs. High accomplishment is in your hands!

Reaching Major Goals Doesn't Happen Overnight

Your razor-sharp determination to get things done is one of the hallmarks of your success. For you, patience has not always been a virtue. In fact, impatience and maintaining a pressing urgency to complete big tasks have actually worked in your favor on the road to attaining major goals.

Inevitably, as you work on projects, particularly big ones, you'll encounter setbacks and obstacles that will delay their completion. While normal, impediments never feel good. But in the end, because you're the person responsible to bring about the anticipated outcome, you're charged to provide the guidance and motivation your staff and volunteers seek to carry them through the ups and downs of making major plans a reality. Your enthusiasm and ability to engender teamwork will make them proud of being part of a goal that is bigger than themselves and will improve the lives of the most vulnerable in the communities they serve.

In the case of my nonprofit, finally seeing the magnificent result of our capital campaign took three years and seven months. At the time, this felt like an eternity. But in retrospect, this was not long at all, given the obstacles I had to deal with and my day-to-day responsibilities, including completing the onboarding tasks described in these Five Frameworks, running the nonprofit, heading a capital campaign within a nonprofit with a scarcity mindset, and overseeing a massive fundraising effort without a consultant. Regarding that last point, I didn't need a consultant because I knew what needed to be done and how to raise money. In addition, because I had clearly defined the campaign's goals and how to reach each one, I was confident I could spearhead the campaign with the support of a solid team and thereby save the nonprofit time and money.

Decades later, seeing how our spectacular headquarters is a huge asset for the community has made dealing with all the ups and downs of the campaign well worth the headaches and effort.

The greatest reward for a program or project you complete is one that operates efficiently and accomplishes exactly what it was designed to do. It is meeting if not exceeding expectations. Course correction to adapt to change, addressing weaknesses, and further reinforcing strengths are part of successful goal attainment.

What your nonprofit has accomplished will open new possibilities to further meet the needs of your community and make your nonprofit stronger and an even bigger force for good. As a result of the pride of being part of reaching a major milestone, your staff and volunteers will look forward to the greater days to come for your nonprofit and playing a role in bringing these about.

Given the rich rewards of a job well done, the immense time and inevitable headaches, bottlenecks, and delays are worthwhile as a means to reach major goals.

Our Nonprofit's Measurements of Success

AT THE END OF OUR EXHAUSTIVELY and impeccably organized status-quo-breaking campaign, we had raised five million dollars and had a turnkey facility with no loans or mortgages! My debt-free obsession was part of capital campaigns for every nonprofit I headed. You could say that being raised in a blue-collar family instilled in me the importance of fiscal responsibility and setting tough but attainable goals.

Our fifty-five-thousand-square-foot standalone headquarters was inviting and accessible to our community members. The campaign covered all costs, including operating the new facility for several years, renovating the existing building, and even acquiring new furnishings. Plus, a foundation donated the land and building to us. Another foundation provided a $250,000 challenge grant match to renovate the building. This motivated a successful local business person. He decided to not only meet that challenge but also create another $250,000 matching challenge in his and his wife's names. His efforts led to yet another entity, along with other corporations in the community, to match that challenge grant. In the end, the donor who sponsored the matching challenge in his and his wife's names provided a seven-figure gift. We, in turn, gave him the naming opportunity for the building.

Leading with an abundance mindset resulted in the community receiving the nonprofit it needed. One way I reached this milestone was through finding new donors, including current corporate partners who were captivated by the capital campaign's promises.

After renovating the building, we hosted a series of celebrations in our new, beautiful headquarters. These events provided our nonprofit memorable public opportunities to honor and recognize the donors, volunteers, construction and design team members, government entities—all that worked tirelessly to push our organization across the finish line. After all the hard work, we could now take a moment to relax and have some fun!

With our new headquarters, we showed our commitment to our community by setting ambitious and pragmatic goals, accomplishing them, and fulfilling our mission to the greatest degree possible. Volunteers and staff saw themselves as winners for pulling off a capital campaign that was previously thought of as downright impossible. In addition, we continued successfully running our other fundraising campaigns. And, most importantly, the health and well-being of our community members improved because we had significantly upgraded the quality of our services. We would face future challenges on local and national issues during my tenure, but this campaign focused us on our mission to serve our community.

Always remember *what* work you perform in taking care of immediate needs is important. But even more so is putting your time and energy toward the more encompassing needs of *who* in your community your nonprofit is charged to serve. As CEO, you serve your community best through having a team that shares your passion for the mission and by providing them the leadership and resources they need.

Every assignment I had as a CEO was meaningful because I was able to realize my vision, fulfill the promises I made to the hiring committee that appointed me, and most importantly, provide the measurement of outcomes that best supported our *who* and the resources used to reach the highest number of people being served. When you're driven by solving the greatest needs in your community, you unleash a potential within you that has the power to rescue society's most vulnerable members and to powerfully affect and save lives.

Chapter 13

Conclusion: Simple Isn't the Same as Easy!

TEN THOUSAND BABY BOOMERS ARE RETIRING every day and will continue to do so through 2030. Many of these boomers exiting the workforce are CEOs, and their vacancies will create a leadership vacuum. You are emerging as a leader during a time of incredible opportunity and promise.

To help deliver on your goals and burning desires to improve and grow the nonprofit you lead is the purpose of this book. In this regard, the Five Frameworks are about teamwork—you'll accomplish your biggest objectives only through building relationships and masterful delegation. You are at the center of creating a remarkable group of staff and volunteers whom you'll count on to realize your vision.

Wanting to do good was what initially motivated you to embark on your nonprofit career journey. To move past altruistic intentions and onto actions that expand an organization's mission beyond what most around you believe possible requires a diverse and specific set of skills and practices. You've learned about these in this book. The Five Frameworks have provided you the roadmap to elevate your leadership to extraordinary heights.

Being a CEO sets you apart from other nonprofit professionals. The Five Frameworks are designed to make your performance and outcomes stand out from this already rarified group of leaders.

Having had a fulfilling and successful professional life, I consider myself fortunate, and I continue to be filled with passion about my industry. Through my work as an entrepreneurial servant leader, I've touched the lives of millions of people. Combined, my fundraising, oversight and analysis, and development efforts throughout my career have resulted in over one billion dollars in human-services funding. Reflecting on the extent to which that dollar amount has improved the lives of people in communities that I have been a part of serving fills me with immense satisfaction. One of the greatest gifts in life is to work in a field that provides you purpose and meaning. The nonprofit sector has provided me an abundance of both. I'm grateful for the growth I've had and life lessons I've learned throughout my career journey.

I've distilled my experience in this book, which is your fast track to high performance. Everything in these pages I've followed, and what you've learned are practices that I've developed through countless hours of work. Along my CEO journey, I've made many mistakes that I learned from and met innumerable obstacles that I overcame. Had I read this book when I started my CEO tenure, I would have spared myself many sleepless nights of nonprofit-induced anxiety!

Thankfully, you won't have to repeat the headaches I've encountered. By following the Five Frameworks, you will experience a meteoric rise in your career without falling into the pitfalls that have stifled the potential, if not stamped out high-accomplishment outright, for those traveling without this comprehensive guide.

You may be tempted to skip steps I've presented, simplify them, or avoid improving areas that reflect weaknesses in your skill set. In this regard, the formula to extraordinary accomplishment is simple: Follow *everything* you've read about here. While you may make modifications that align with the particular structure of your nonprofit, doing so is not the same as creating shortcuts.

Simple isn't the same as easy. Following the Five Frameworks is a simple requirement, yet far from effortless. But the tangible results you'll experience will be worthwhile rewards for your focused effort.

As the coronavirus has taught us, global health crises, geopolitics, technology, and natural as well as human-made catastrophes can disrupt our lives for weeks, months, and years. The Five Frameworks are a timeless guide to high achievement during periods of rapid change that will only accelerate over the years to come. Lead with conviction and confidence knowing that following what you've learned in these pages will pour the strong foundation necessary to achieve greatness throughout your CEO journey.

Notes

Chapter 1

5   **"the turnover in nonprofit corner offices is between 18% and 22% annually."**   "Nonprofit Executive Director Turnover—Not If, but When," Jacobson Jarvis & Co., June 15, 2019, https://jjco.com/2019/06/15/nonprofit-executive-director-turnover-not-if-but-when/.

5   **CEOs are in their roles for an average of six years**   Emily H. Benham, "2021 State of the Nonprofit Sector: The Painful, the Extraordinary and What's Next," NLC, October 13, 2021, https://nlctb.org/news/2021-state-of-the-nonprofit-sector/.

6   **the typical two consecutive three-year terms**   "Nonprofit Executive Director Turnover—Not If, but When," Jacobson Jarvis & Co., June 15, 2019, https://jjco.com/2019/06/15/nonprofit-executive-director-turnover-not-if-but-when/.

Chapter 2

11   *one-third to one-half of new CEOs fail*   Dan Ciampa, "After the Handshake," *Harvard Business Review*, December 2016, https://hbr.org/2016/12/after-the-handshake.

11   **1. A CEO's insufficient skill set.**   Tracy Vanderneck, "It Takes a Great Leader: CEOs Can Make or Break Nonprofit Organizations," NonProfitPRO, February 6, 2018, https://www.nonprofitpro.com/article/takes-great-leader-ceos-can-make-break-nonprofit-organizations/.

11   **2. Conflicts between CEOs and boards.**   Emily Wilson and Melanie Lockwood Herman, "Clash of the Nonprofit Titans: Managing Board and CEO Conflicts," Nonprofit Risk Management Center, accessed November 7, 2022, https://nonprofitrisk.org/resources/articles/clash-of-the-nonprofit-titans-managing-board-and-ceo-conflicts/.

12   **3. Not clearly stating the organization's mission, purpose, and structure.**   "7 Deadly Sins of Nonprofit Failure and How to Avoid Them," NPCrowd, accessed November 7, 2022, https://npcrowd.com/7-deadly-sins-of-nonprofit-failure-avoid/#2-losing-your-way-without-core-values-and-a-singular-mission-.

12   **6. An outdated or non-existent long-term strategic plan.**   Tracy S. Ebarb, "Nonprofits Fail—Here's Seven Reasons Why," NANOE, September 7, 2019, https://nanoe.org/nonprofits-fail/.

13   **7. Poor financial practices.**   Tracy S. Ebarb, "Nonprofits Fail—Here's Seven Reasons Why," NANOE, September 7, 2019, https://nanoe.org/nonprofits-fail/.

13   **8. Inadequate technology infrastructure.** Tracy S. Ebarb, "Nonprofits Fail—Here's Seven Reasons Why," NANOE, September 7, 2019, https://nanoe.org/nonprofits-fail/.

14   **"Successors to long serving CEOs** "CEO Turnover at Record High; Successors Following Long Serving CEOs Struggling According to PwC's Strategy & Global Study," PwC, accessed November 7, 2022, https://www.pwc.com/gx/en/news-room/press-releases/2019/ceo-turnover-record-high.html.

Chapter 6

73   **more than seventy-seven million Americans** "Key Findings from the 2019 Current Population Survey: Civic Engagement and Volunteering Supplement," AmeriCorps Research and Evaluation, December 2021, https://americorps.gov/sites/default/files/document/2019%20CPS%20CEV%20findings%20report%20CLEAN_10Dec2021_508.pdf.

73   **1.54 million charitable organizations in the United States** "The Nonprofit Sector in Brief 2019," Urban Institute, June 4, 2020, https://nccs.urban.org/publication/nonprofit-sector-brief-2019.

75   **while growing up, their parents modeled philanthropy** "How and Why Women Give: Current and Future Directions for Research on Women's Philanthropy," IUPUI Women's Philanthropy Institute, May 2015, https://wnywomensfoundation.org/app/uploads/2017/08/6.-How-and-Why-Women-Give.pdf.

75   **56 percent of US adults donated** Dawn Papandrea, "56% of Americans Donated to Charity in 2021, at Average of $574," LendingTree, updated November 29, 2021, https://www.lendingtree.com/debt-consolidation/charitable-donations-survey-study/.

75 **corporations gave $21 billion** Esther Larson, "Giving USA Report Shows 2021 Charitable Giving Strong, but Did Not Keep Pace with Inflation," Philanthropy Roundtable, June 27, 2022, https://www.philanthropyroundtable.org/giving-usa-report-shows-2021-charitable-giving-strong-but-did-not-keep-pace-with-inflation/.

Chapter 10

172 **Some states also specify that nonprofits receiving public funding** "State Law Nonprofit Audit Requirements," National Council of Nonprofits, updated August 2022, https://www.councilofnonprofits.org/nonprofit-audit-guide/state-law-audit-requirements.

172 **if the nonprofit receives more than $750,000** "Does Your Nonprofit Need to Have an Independent Audit?" National Council of Nonprofits, accessed November 7, 2022, https://www.councilofnonprofits.org/nonprofit-audit-guide/need-independent-audit.

Chapter 12

244 **Linton Allen** George W. Koehn, "Community Banks Shaped Orlando: Advisory Board," *Orlando Sentinel*, November 28, 2015, https://www.orlandosentinel.com/opinion/os-ed-community-banks-advisory-board-112915-20151127-story.html.

Chapter 13

253 **Ten thousand baby boomers** Glenn Kessler, "Do 10,000 Baby Boomers Retire Every Day?" *Washington Post*, July 24, 2014, https://www.washingtonpost.com/news/fact-checker/wp/2014/07/24/do-10000-baby-boomers-retire-every-day/.

Learn More about the Five Frameworks

IF YOUR NONPROFIT IS ONBOARDING A new CEO, you need help.

And if you don't have a new CEO, you likely soon will. A nonprofit's board of directors can expect to navigate a leadership change every five years. It usually takes over a year before new CEOs fully contribute to and assimilate into nonprofits. Plus it takes at least ten months and usually longer to recruit a new CEO—often at a cost of tens of thousands of dollars and countless hours of time. Plus, every year, employee turnover within nonprofits is 20 percent.

But why does turnover happen so often in the first place? The great news is that it doesn't have to be this way.

Brian Quail Executive Consulting provides transitional executive coaching for nonprofit CEOs. The result is improved onboarding, longer and more successful tenures, reduced stress and burnout, and significant and immediate improvements that provide long-term benefit to the nonprofit.

With a career spanning four decades in nonprofits and twenty-five years as a CEO, Brian is expertly equipped to guide you on your journey of high achievement. As a keynote speaker, as a facilitator for workshops and seminars, and in one-on-one engagements for new CEOs and boards, Brian will help you deliver remarkable results for your mission-critical work. To learn more, visit www.BrianQuail.com.

To purchase additional copies of *The Ultimate Guide for New Nonprofit CEOs*, go to Amazon.com.

About the Author

BRIAN QUAIL IS FOUNDER AND CEO of Quail Consulting, which focuses on guiding nonprofit CEOs and boards to achieve exceptional results. His nonprofit career spanned four decades, including twenty-five years serving as CEO of three affiliates of national organizations: Heart of Florida United Way, American Red Cross Louisville Area Chapter, and Boys & Girls Clubs of Broward County. Combined, his fundraising, oversight, analysis, and development efforts throughout his professional life have resulted in over one billion dollars in human-services funding.

Born in Clinton and raised in neighboring Sterling, Massachusetts, Brian attributes his discipline and integrity to his hard-working blue-collar parents. After graduating from the University of Massachusetts Amherst, he went on to the University of Chicago where he earned his MA in nonprofit administration and management in 1984.

Since 2009, he and his wonderful wife, Liz, have called Fort Lauderdale, Florida, home. There he enjoys spending time with their amazing daughter, Chloe, running his consulting and speaking services, volunteering, fitness training, playing golf, and attending sporting events.

Made in the USA
Monee, IL
16 August 2023